STAND & WITHSTAND INTEGRITY GROUP PRE

THE DEMAND

EDUCATION REFORM WE NEED
INITIATED BY THE STUDENTS WE LEAD

Library of Congress Cataloging-in-Publication Data has been applied for.
ISBN 978-1-7369736-4-6 (Paperback)

Printed in the United States of America

First Edition October 2021

P.O. Box 782771
Wichita, KS 67278
STANDWITHSTAND.ORG

CONTENTS

HOW DO I USE THIS JOURNAL?

As a student, it is of the utmost importance that you possess, understand, know how to use, and benefit from materials and tools designed to assist you in pursuing an education. This journal is to serve as an additional resource to *Demand It: What "Go to School and Get an Education" Really Means.* While reading that book, the relevance, significance, and importance of allies should have been made clear to you. You were informed that:

> "Your ability to answer the two never-ending, afterschool questions is a clear indication of how well you have judged and inventoried the results of the educational opportunities that your school provided you. "How was school today," or "What did you learn at school today," may seem like parental small talk, but they are powerfully reflective questions that ask you to make sure you have what you went to school to get… You can no longer look at these questions as though they are meaningless chitchat, attempts to be nosey, or pushy interrogations. These are opportunities to strengthen the bond of the alliance."

You owe it to yourself, being the only person who can assess the quality of your educational experience and hold teachers accountable for educating, to answer these questions. Use 20-30 minutes (less time will be needed when this becomes a daily activity) to reflect and fill out your journal each day. Doing so will make it nearly impossible for you to be cheated out of the education the system says it wants for you. With *that* kind of potential, your allies should also have regular access to this journal. In doing so, you are documenting the happenings of your K-12 experience and a catalogued inventory of the education you acquire. Looking up at the end of a semester, school year, or a K-12 academic career and discovering you missed out on an education is a frightening position to be in. Do not allow this to happen to you!

How Was School Today?

What parents and allies are really saying when they ask this question is, "Tell me about the best, worst, and disinteresting parts of your day so that I can judge whether or not my assistance could be of service to you in some way." What may, to you, seem to be unimportant or meaningless in the grand scheme of things, could be worth a second look or critical examination when an invested ally is made aware. This one question, "How Was School Today," is really a combination of six different questions that need to be considered in the following ways as you document the happenings of your day:

1) <u>How did you get along with people? – Circle the options that best represent your experience.</u>
   Allies = individuals I care for and believe they care for me.

   Annoyances = individuals I do not particularly care for or believe they care for me.

   Instructors = collective staff, faculty members, and adults I interact with throughout the day.

   Positive = the collective interactions with this people group were seen as beneficial for the day.

   Negative = the collective interactions with this people group were seen as undesirable for the day.

   Neutral = the collective interactions with this people group were seen as typical for the day.

HOW DO I USE THIS JOURNAL?

2) <u>How did you behave? – Circle the options that best represent your experience.</u>

Successes = actions, behaviors, and/or conversations that exceed typical expectations.

Struggles = actions, behaviors, and/or conversations that fell below typical expectations.

Confessions = mistakes I have made that I am tempted to lie about or keep secret for fear of trouble.

Major = three or more in quantity, excellent in quality.

Minor = one or two in quantity, better than average in quality.

None = nothing happened; nothing worth mentioning.

3) <u>How was your energy? – Circle the options that best represent your experience.</u>

Morning = from the time I wake up to the class before lunch.

Noon = from the class before lunch to the end of my lunch period.

Afternoon = from the end of my lunch period to the end of school dismissal bell.

Full Tank = enough energy to do what needs to be done at a high level, and then some.

Half Tank = enough energy to do what needs to be done the way it needs to be done.

Empty = not enough energy to do what needs to be done the way it needs to be done.

4) <u>Did you need the nurse? – Circle the options that best represent your experience.</u>

Health = a situation concerning my overall well-being.

Injury = a situation concerning me hurting something specific.

Pain = a situation concerning discomfort that I cannot really explain.

Yes = the nurse was needed.

No = the nurse was not needed

5) <u>How was the food? – Circle the options that best represent your experience.</u>

Breakfast = meal meant to be eaten before the school day begins.

Lunch = meal meant to be eaten between morning and afternoon classes.

Snacks = any item(s) that are eaten between meals.

Delicious = a meal I enjoy eating that is tasty, balanced, and filling (3 of 3).

Decent = a meal I can appreciate due to it being tasty, balanced, or filling (at least 1 of 3).

Disgusting = a meal with undesirable taste, insufficient balance, or small portions (at least 2 of 3).

Didn't Eat = no meal eaten.

6) <u>How was your day? – Write the letter B, W, or M on the emoji representing that part of your day.</u>

Best = the part of my day that was preferred over all others.

Worst = the part of my day that was least pleasant.

Most = how did I feel consistently about/throughout my day.

(Note: one emoji *can* hold multiple letters for the day.)

HOW DO I USE THIS JOURNAL?

What Did You Learn Today?

What parents and allies are really saying when they ask this question is, "Tell me how your classes are going and how your instructors are doing so that I can judge whether or not my assistance could be of service to you in some way." What may, to you, seem to be unimportant or meaningless in the grand scheme of things, could be worth a second look or critical examination when an invested ally is made aware. This one question, "What Did You Learn Today," is really a combination of five different questions that need to be considered in the following ways as you document the happenings of your day:

1) <u>What level/type of engagement did your classes require of you today?</u>
   In this section, list the classes you attended under the "**IN THIS CLASS**" column. Then, identify the most common way(s) each class had you participate in your own education that day.

   Thinking = my mind was an active tool for what was done in class.

   Seeing = my eyes were an active tool for what was done in class.

   Listening = my ears were an active tool for what was done in class.

   Doing = my hands (writing), mouth (talking), or other body part (movement/activity) was an active tool for what was done in class.

2) <u>What was the educational value of what your classes offered you today?</u>
   In this section, list the classes you attended under the "**THIS CLASS**" column. Then, write which Minimum Functionality(s) and Maximum Possibility(s) each class focused on. Write the category number first (1-10), then the specific type from that category (ex. #3 - Landscape Architect). Review the Educational Value Continuum™ and ask your teacher directly if you cannot figure out the educational value of a lesson. This is your most demanding reflection task. Take careful time to review the Educational Value Continuum™, remember the class experience, and record, to the best of your ability, the most important component of your education. The more you do this, the more trained you are in recognizing the educational value of a lesson, the easier this task will become.

3) <u>How would you rate the overall performance of your instructors today?</u>
   Compare the overall effectiveness of each instructor in your attended classes and decide what their performance most aligned your experience with. This section is assessing the instructor more than it is the class/content. Once you decide, write the instructors name under the "**THIS INSTRUCTOR**" column that you believe to have done the most of the following:

   Education = focus on educational components 3 and 4 and/or the Educational Value Continuum™.

   Teaching = focus on educational components 1 and 2 and/or dull task that felt like "busy work".

   Fun = focus on enjoying the experience of whatever may have been the goal.

   Challenges = presented an educational experience that was difficult and pushed me beyond comfort.
   (Note: one teacher *can* hold multiple slots for the day, but only one teacher per slot.)

4) <u>What kind of issues did you have while pursuing your education today?</u>
   In this section, you will identify academic struggles that come up. In the "**BROUGHT ME THE MOST ISSUES**" column, write down which class, concept, lesson, and instructor presented you with the most conflict. While pursuing an education, different issues occur for different reasons. To prevent them from becoming larger or ongoing problems, tell your allies when you have trouble with a:

HOW DO I USE THIS JOURNAL?

Class = curriculum, organization, or feel of a course seems off or feels overwhelming entirely.

Concept = as it was taught or understood, making sense of a specific question, topic, or idea was difficult to do.

Lesson = as it was taught or understood, making sense of an entire segment of a class session was difficult to do.

Instructor = problems due to personality, teaching methods, expectations, or a disagreement.

(Note: "none" is an acceptable answer if this was your genuine experience for the day.)

5) <u>How would you rate the overall quality of your classes today?</u>
Compare the educational value and overall experience of each of your attended classes and decide what the experience in each one was most connected to. This section is assessing the class/content more than it is the instructor. Once you decide, indicate which of your classes was the most:

Educational = emphasis on educational components 3 and 4 and/or the Educational Value Continuum™.

Work = emphasis on educational components 1 and 2 and/or dull task resembling "busy work".

Fun = emphasis on enjoying the experience of whatever may have been the focus.

Boring = emphasis on work/tasks that were not enjoyable and difficult to assess as educational.

(Note: one class *can* hold multiple slots for the day, but only one class per slot.)

Progress Report:

Over the course of a nine-week period, much activity, learning, growth, and educating *should* be occurring. A full schoolyear offers too much to grasp an understanding of at the year's end. Failing to keep record of the daily happenings of your school days will allow for semesters, school years, and academic levels to pass with no evidence of learning. By reflecting on your record every quarter and taking note of patterns and trends as they occur, you will be able to make adjustments as needed and maximize your educational experience. Complete these ten statements with information that applies based on your careful consideration of the recorded daily notes from your nine-week experience:

1) When I think about my interactions with people this quarter, I see that…
2) When I think about my behavior this quarter, I see that…
3) When I think about my overall health this quarter, I see that…
4) When I think about my eating habits this quarter, I see that…
5) When I think about my overall experience in school this quarter, I see that…
6) When I think about the different issues I had this quarter, I see that…
7) When I think about the educational value of class experiences this quarter, I see that…
8) When I think about how my instructors did this quarter, I see that…
9) When I think about academic issues I had this quarter, I see that…
10) When I think about how my classes went this quarter, I see that…

While reflecting, consider each of these four aspects for each of the ten statements as they apply:

1) I was successful… – what went well consistently, where did you shine, keep the good things going?
2) I really struggled… – what is not working, where are you stressed, where are improvements needed?
3) Moving forward… – what adjustments should be made to classes, instructors, relationships, habits, etc.?
4) I need my allies… – feeling incapable, unheard, unsafe, or unproductive in any area; what help do you need?

EDUCATIONAL VALUE CONTINUUM™

Minimum Functionality:

On the most basic level, what purpose does the study of this subject and support material serve in my life (now or in the foreseeable future) that benefits me directly?

1) **Ability** – offers the power or capability to do.
   Learners Say: "I now know how to ____ and can ____."
   Example: "I now know how to compose a thesis statement and can articulate a strong argument or stance for any opinion I have."

2) **Skill** – raises the level and proficiency of an ability already possessed.
   Learners Say: "I am now better at ____."
   Example: "I am now better at supporting my personal opinion with evidence from credible sources."

3) **Vocation** – develops the understanding of a certain job, profession, or business.
   Learners Say: "I now know (what / what a) ____ (are / is) and (do / does)."
   Example: "I now know what an anesthesiologist is and does."

4) **Relationship** – develops the understanding of human connection, interaction, and involvement.
   Learners Say: "I can now (relate better to / better understand the / more easily) ____ because of ____."
   Example: "I can now relate better to people who are different because of a lesson on World War II and the Holocaust."

5) **Mentality** – challenges, changes, composes, or confirms personal perspectives on life or the world.
   Learners Say: "My ideas about ____ (are now / have been) ____ due to ____."
   Example: "My ideas about gun control are now more progressive due to mass shooting statistics."

6) **Mental Exercise** – works, conditions, or trains the brain for better overall functionality.
   Learners Say: "I am able (to / to do) ____ (better / more) because I have exercised my mind."
   Example: "I am able to make rational decisions more quickly because I have exercised my mind."

7) **Muscle Memory** – works, conditions, or trains the physical body for better overall functionality.
   Learners Say: "I am able (to / to do) ____ (better / more) ____ because I have exercised my body."
   Example: "I am able to be active without pain or fatigue more because I have exercised my body."

8) **Practice** – provides time and opportunity to raise competence or effectiveness of an ability.
   Learners Say: "I worked to improve my ____ by ____."
   Example: "I worked to improve my diction and ability to project by doing vocal warmups in choir."

9) **Training** – provides purposeful, more disciplined, focused, and intensive practice of a specific ability to become more skilled.
   Learners Say: "I worked to improve my ____ by ____."
   Example: "I worked to improve my attention to detail by measuring ingredients for a recipe."

10) **Experience** – encountering and becoming more familiar in order to raise one's awareness or aptitude.
    Learners Say: "I spent time ____ to be (better / more) ____ (at / with / of) ____."
    Example: "I spent time working with a group to be more knowledgeable of how well people with different personalities can work together."

EDUCATIONAL VALUE CONTINUUM™

Maximum Possibility:

At the most accomplished and advanced level, what purpose could the study of this subject and support material serve in my life and what beneficial position could it ultimately land me in?

1) **Motivation** – creates or causes a reason to act.
   Learners Say: "I now have a (desire / stronger desire) to ____."
   Example: "I now have a stronger desire to manage my finances well enough to retire young."

2) **Inspiration** – sparks or ignites an internal motivation.
   Learners Say: "I feel ____ compelling me to ____."
   Example: "I feel the restrictions on past generations compelling me to surpass what limited them."

3) **Higher Education** – instills the desire to pursue an education past the high school level.
   Learners Say: "I want to go to ____ and study ____ (to / so that) ____."
   Example: "I want to go to art school and study graphic design so that I can start my own branding company."

4) **Career** – instills the desire to pursue a specific profession or occupation.
   Learners Say: "I want to (be a / work for) ____ so that I can ____."
   Example: "I want to be a zoologist so that I can work with endangered populations."

5) **Dream** – instills the desire to pursue a grandiose goal, passion, or vision.
   Learners Say: "I want (to / to be) ____ and one day ____."
   Example: "I want to be a marine and one day become Sergeant Major of the Marine Corps."

6) **Invention** – stimulates the imagination to create something that did not exist previously.
   Learners Say: "I want to create (a / the) ____ that (can / will) ____."
   Example: "I want to create a waste disposal method that will be good for the environment."

7) **Innovation** – stimulates the imagination to create something newer than the already established.
   Learners Say: "I want to improve ____ so that (it / it can) ____."
   Example: "I want to improve solar technology so that it can help fight against climate change."

8) **Non-Profit** – motivates one to establish, develop, and pursue goals meant to provide a public service or benefit.
   Learners Say: "I want to help ____ so they will be able to ____."
   Example: "I want to help the homeless so they will be able to live stable and productive lives."

9) **Fortune-500** – motivates one to establish, develop, and pursue goals meant to gain significant financial wealth.
   Learners Say: "I want to become ____ and acquire ____."
   Example: "I want to become CEO of a major corporation and acquire 7-figure gains annually."

10) **Superhero** – motivates one to establish, develop, and pursue goals meant to effect positive change on the largest possible scale.
   Learners Say: "I want to impact and improve ____ by ____."
   Example: "I want to impact and improve the probability of people living fulfilled lives by helping them to secure for themselves a high-quality education at the earliest possible age."

DEDICATION:

To every child who was ever asked, "How was school today," or, "What did you learn today," and every adult who ever asked those questions. Allow this journal to help you to improve that conversation.

STUDENT NAME / GRADE / SCHOOL NAME

SCHOOL YEAR

20 ___ / ___ 20 ___

QUARTER

FIRST   SECOND   THIRD   FOURTH

CLASS SCHEDULE

CLASS	TEACHER	ROOM #	TIME

RECORD IT
HOW WAS SCHOOL TODAY?

DATE: _____

HOW DID YOU GET ALONG WITH PEOPLE?

ALLIES: POSITIVE / NEGATIVE / NEUTRAL

ANNOYANCES: POSITIVE / NEGATIVE / NEUTRAL   INSTRUCTORS: POSITIVE / NEGATIVE / NEUTRAL

HOW DID YOU BEHAVE?

SUCCESSES: MAJOR / MINOR / NONE

STRUGGLES: MAJOR / MINOR / NONE

CONFESSIONS: MAJOR / MINOR / NONE

HOW WAS YOUR ENERGY?

MORNING: FULL TANK / HALF TANK / EMPTY   NOON: FULL TANK / HALF TANK / EMPTY

AFTERNOON: FULL TANK / HALF TANK / EMPTY

DID YOU NEED THE NURSE?

HEALTH: YES / NO   INJURY: YES / NO   PAIN: YES / NO

HOW WAS THE FOOD?

BREAKFAST: DELICIOUS / DECENT / DISGUSTING / DIDN'T EAT

LUNCH: DELICIOUS / DECENT / DISGUSTING / DIDN'T EAT

SNACKS: DELICIOUS / DECENT / DISGUSTING / DIDN'T EAT

QUIET   ANNOYED   COOL   SAD   TIRED   EXCITED   HAPPY   EMBARRASSED   SCARED

BORED   SICK   FRUSTRATED   ANGRY   FUNNY   PROUD   NERVOUS   GOOFY   SURPRISED

B = BEST PART OF YOUR DAY   W = WORST PART OF YOUR DAY   M = MOST OF THE DAY

RECORD IT
WHAT DID YOU LEARN TODAY?

MINIMUM FUNCTIONALITY

1) ABILITY	2) SKILL	3) VOCATION	4) RELATIONSHIP	5) MENTALITY
6) MENTAL EXERCISE	7) MUSCLE MEMORY	8) PRACTICE	9) TRAINING	10) EXPERIENCE

IN THIS CLASS	I ENGAGED MOST BY...		MINIMUM FUNCTIONALITY	THIS CLASS	MAXIMUM POSSIBILITY
	THINKING SEEING LISTENING DOING				
	THINKING SEEING LISTENING DOING				
	THINKING SEEING LISTENING DOING				
	THINKING SEEING LISTENING DOING				
	THINKING SEEING LISTENING DOING				
	THINKING SEEING LISTENING DOING				
	THINKING SEEING LISTENING DOING				
	THINKING SEEING LISTENING DOING				

THIS INSTRUCTOR	BROUGHT ME THE MOST...
	EDUCATION
	TEACHING
	FUN
	CHALLENGES

THIS...	BROUGHT ME THE MOST ISSUES
CLASS	
CONCEPT	
LESSON	
INSTRUCTOR	

THIS CLASS	WAS THE MOST...
	EDUCATIONAL
	WORK
	FUN
	BORING

MAXIMUM POSSIBILITY

1) MOTIVATION	2) INSPIRATION	3) HIGHER EDUCATION	4) CAREER	5) DREAM
6) INVENTION	7) INNOVATION	8) NON-PROFIT	9) FORTUNE 500	10) SUPERHERO

RECORD IT
How Was School Today?

DATE:_____

HOW DID YOU GET ALONG WITH PEOPLE?

ALLIES: POSITIVE / NEGATIVE / NEUTRAL

ANNOYANCES: POSITIVE / NEGATIVE / NEUTRAL   INSTRUCTORS: POSITIVE / NEGATIVE / NEUTRAL

HOW DID YOU BEHAVE?

SUCCESSES: MAJOR / MINOR / NONE

STRUGGLES: MAJOR / MINOR / NONE

CONFESSIONS: MAJOR / MINOR / NONE

HOW WAS YOUR ENERGY?

MORNING: FULL TANK / HALF TANK / EMPTY   NOON: FULL TANK / HALF TANK / EMPTY

AFTERNOON: FULL TANK / HALF TANK / EMPTY

DID YOU NEED THE NURSE?

HEALTH: YES / NO   INJURY: YES / NO   PAIN: YES / NO

HOW WAS THE FOOD?

BREAKFAST: DELICIOUS / DECENT / DISGUSTING / DIDN'T EAT

LUNCH: DELICIOUS / DECENT / DISGUSTING / DIDN'T EAT

SNACKS: DELICIOUS / DECENT / DISGUSTING / DIDN'T EAT

QUIET   ANNOYED   COOL   SAD   TIRED   EXCITED   HAPPY   EMBARRASSED   SCARED

BORED   SICK   FRUSTRATED   ANGRY   FUNNY   PROUD   NERVOUS   GOOFY   SURPRISED

B = BEST PART OF YOUR DAY   **W** = WORST PART OF YOUR DAY   **M** = MOST OF THE DAY

RECORD IT
WHAT DID YOU LEARN TODAY?

MINIMUM FUNCTIONALITY

1) ABILITY	2) SKILL	3) VOCATION	4) RELATIONSHIP	5) MENTALITY
6) MENTAL EXERCISE	7) MUSCLE MEMORY	8) PRACTICE	9) TRAINING	10) EXPERIENCE

IN THIS CLASS	I ENGAGED MOST BY ...	MINIMUM FUNCTIONALITY	THIS CLASS	MAXIMUM POSSIBILITY
	THINKING SEEING LISTENING DOING			
	THINKING SEEING LISTENING DOING			
	THINKING SEEING LISTENING DOING			
	THINKING SEEING LISTENING DOING			
	THINKING SEEING LISTENING DOING			
	THINKING SEEING LISTENING DOING			
	THINKING SEEING LISTENING DOING			
	THINKING SEEING LISTENING DOING			

THIS INSTRUCTOR	BROUGHT ME THE MOST...
	EDUCATION
	TEACHING
	FUN
	CHALLENGES

THIS...	BROUGHT ME THE MOST ISSUES
CLASS	
CONCEPT	
LESSON	
INSTRUCTOR	

THIS CLASS	WAS THE MOST...
	EDUCATIONAL
	WORK
	FUN
	BORING

MAXIMUM POSSIBILITY

1) MOTIVATION	2) INSPIRATION	3) HIGHER EDUCATION	4) CAREER	5) DREAM
6) INVENTION	7) INNOVATION	8) NON-PROFIT	9) FORTUNE 500	10) SUPERHERO

How Was School Today?

DATE:_____

HOW DID YOU GET ALONG WITH PEOPLE?

ALLIES: POSITIVE / NEGATIVE / NEUTRAL

ANNOYANCES: POSITIVE / NEGATIVE / NEUTRAL   INSTRUCTORS: POSITIVE / NEGATIVE / NEUTRAL

HOW DID YOU BEHAVE?

SUCCESSES: MAJOR / MINOR / NONE

STRUGGLES: MAJOR / MINOR / NONE

CONFESSIONS: MAJOR / MINOR / NONE

HOW WAS YOUR ENERGY?

MORNING: FULL TANK / HALF TANK / EMPTY   NOON: FULL TANK / HALF TANK / EMPTY

AFTERNOON: FULL TANK / HALF TANK / EMPTY

DID YOU NEED THE NURSE?

HEALTH: YES / NO   INJURY: YES / NO   PAIN: YES / NO

HOW WAS THE FOOD?

BREAKFAST: DELICIOUS / DECENT / DISGUSTING / DIDN'T EAT

LUNCH: DELICIOUS / DECENT / DISGUSTING / DIDN'T EAT

SNACKS: DELICIOUS / DECENT / DISGUSTING / DIDN'T EAT

QUIET   ANNOYED   COOL   SAD   TIRED   EXCITED   HAPPY   EMBARRASSED   SCARED

BORED   SICK   FRUSTRATED   ANGRY   FUNNY   PROUD   NERVOUS   GOOFY   SURPRISED

B = BEST PART OF YOUR DAY   **W** = WORST PART OF YOUR DAY   **M** = MOST OF THE DAY

RECORD IT
WHAT DID YOU LEARN TODAY?

MINIMUM FUNCTIONALITY

1) ABILITY	2) SKILL	3) VOCATION	4) RELATIONSHIP	5) MENTALITY
6) MENTAL EXERCISE	7) MUSCLE MEMORY	8) PRACTICE	9) TRAINING	10) EXPERIENCE

IN THIS CLASS	I ENGAGED MOST BY ...	MINIMUM FUNCTIONALITY	THIS CLASS	MAXIMUM POSSIBILITY
	THINKING SEEING LISTENING DOING			
	THINKING SEEING LISTENING DOING			
	THINKING SEEING LISTENING DOING			
	THINKING SEEING LISTENING DOING			
	THINKING SEEING LISTENING DOING			
	THINKING SEEING LISTENING DOING			
	THINKING SEEING LISTENING DOING			
	THINKING SEEING LISTENING DOING			

THIS INSTRUCTOR	BROUGHT ME THE MOST...
	EDUCATION
	TEACHING
	FUN
	CHALLENGES

THIS...	BROUGHT ME THE MOST ISSUES
CLASS	
CONCEPT	
LESSON	
INSTRUCTOR	

THIS CLASS	WAS THE MOST...
	EDUCATIONAL
	WORK
	FUN
	BORING

MAXIMUM POSSIBILITY

1) MOTIVATION	2) INSPIRATION	3) HIGHER EDUCATION	4) CAREER	5) DREAM
6) INVENTION	7) INNOVATION	8) NON-PROFIT	9) FORTUNE 500	10) SUPERHERO

RECORD IT
How Was School Today?

DATE:_____

HOW DID YOU GET ALONG WITH PEOPLE?

ALLIES: POSITIVE / NEGATIVE / NEUTRAL

ANNOYANCES: POSITIVE / NEGATIVE / NEUTRAL   INSTRUCTORS: POSITIVE / NEGATIVE / NEUTRAL

HOW DID YOU BEHAVE?

SUCCESSES: MAJOR / MINOR / NONE

STRUGGLES: MAJOR / MINOR / NONE

CONFESSIONS: MAJOR / MINOR / NONE

HOW WAS YOUR ENERGY?

MORNING: FULL TANK / HALF TANK / EMPTY   NOON: FULL TANK / HALF TANK / EMPTY

AFTERNOON: FULL TANK / HALF TANK / EMPTY

DID YOU NEED THE NURSE?

HEALTH: YES / NO   INJURY: YES / NO   PAIN: YES / NO

HOW WAS THE FOOD?

BREAKFAST: DELICIOUS / DECENT / DISGUSTING / DIDN'T EAT

LUNCH: DELICIOUS / DECENT / DISGUSTING / DIDN'T EAT

SNACKS: DELICIOUS / DECENT / DISGUSTING / DIDN'T EAT

QUIET   ANNOYED   COOL   SAD   TIRED   EXCITED   HAPPY   EMBARRASSED   SCARED

BORED   SICK   FRUSTRATED   ANGRY   FUNNY   PROUD   NERVOUS   GOOFY   SURPRISED

B = BEST PART OF YOUR DAY   W = WORST PART OF YOUR DAY   M = MOST OF THE DAY

RECORD IT
WHAT DID YOU LEARN TODAY?

1) ABILITY	2) SKILL	3) VOCATION	4) RELATIONSHIP	5) MENTALITY
6) MENTAL EXERCISE	7) MUSCLE MEMORY	8) PRACTICE	9) TRAINING	10) EXPERIENCE

IN THIS CLASS	I ENGAGED MOST BY …		MINIMUM FUNCTIONALITY	THIS CLASS	MAXIMUM POSSIBILITY
	THINKING SEEING LISTENING DOING				
	THINKING SEEING LISTENING DOING				
	THINKING SEEING LISTENING DOING				
	THINKING SEEING LISTENING DOING				
	THINKING SEEING LISTENING DOING				
	THINKING SEEING LISTENING DOING				
	THINKING SEEING LISTENING DOING				
	THINKING SEEING LISTENING DOING				

THIS INSTRUCTOR	BROUGHT ME THE MOST…
	EDUCATION
	TEACHING
	FUN
	CHALLENGES

THIS…	BROUGHT ME THE MOST ISSUES
CLASS	
CONCEPT	
LESSON	
INSTRUCTOR	

THIS CLASS	WAS THE MOST…
	EDUCATIONAL
	WORK
	FUN
	BORING

MAXIMUM POSSIBILITY

1) MOTIVATION	2) INSPIRATION	3) HIGHER EDUCATION	4) CAREER	5) DREAM
6) INVENTION	7) INNOVATION	8) NON-PROFIT	9) FORTUNE 500	10) SUPERHERO

HOW WAS SCHOOL TODAY?

DATE: _____

HOW DID YOU GET ALONG WITH PEOPLE?

ALLIES: POSITIVE / NEGATIVE / NEUTRAL

ANNOYANCES: POSITIVE / NEGATIVE / NEUTRAL   INSTRUCTORS: POSITIVE / NEGATIVE / NEUTRAL

HOW DID YOU BEHAVE?

SUCCESSES: MAJOR / MINOR / NONE

STRUGGLES: MAJOR / MINOR / NONE

CONFESSIONS: MAJOR / MINOR / NONE

HOW WAS YOUR ENERGY?

MORNING: FULL TANK / HALF TANK / EMPTY   NOON: FULL TANK / HALF TANK / EMPTY

AFTERNOON: FULL TANK / HALF TANK / EMPTY

DID YOU NEED THE NURSE?

HEALTH: YES / NO   INJURY: YES / NO   PAIN: YES / NO

HOW WAS THE FOOD?

BREAKFAST: DELICIOUS / DECENT / DISGUSTING / DIDN'T EAT

LUNCH: DELICIOUS / DECENT / DISGUSTING / DIDN'T EAT

SNACKS: DELICIOUS / DECENT / DISGUSTING / DIDN'T EAT

QUIET   ANNOYED   COOL   SAD   TIRED   EXCITED   HAPPY   EMBARRASSED   SCARED

BORED   SICK   FRUSTRATED   ANGRY   FUNNY   PROUD   NERVOUS   GOOFY   SURPRISED

B = BEST PART OF YOUR DAY   **W** = WORST PART OF YOUR DAY   **M** = MOST OF THE DAY

RECORD IT
WHAT DID YOU LEARN TODAY?

MINIMUM FUNCTIONALITY

1) ABILITY	2) SKILL	3) VOCATION	4) RELATIONSHIP	5) MENTALITY
6) MENTAL EXERCISE	7) MUSCLE MEMORY	8) PRACTICE	9) TRAINING	10) EXPERIENCE

IN THIS CLASS	I ENGAGED MOST BY ...	MINIMUM FUNCTIONALITY	THIS CLASS	MAXIMUM POSSIBILITY
	THINKING SEEING LISTENING DOING			
	THINKING SEEING LISTENING DOING			
	THINKING SEEING LISTENING DOING			
	THINKING SEEING LISTENING DOING			
	THINKING SEEING LISTENING DOING			
	THINKING SEEING LISTENING DOING			
	THINKING SEEING LISTENING DOING			
	THINKING SEEING LISTENING DOING			

THIS INSTRUCTOR	BROUGHT ME THE MOST...
	EDUCATION
	TEACHING
	FUN
	CHALLENGES

THIS...	BROUGHT ME THE MOST ISSUES
CLASS	
CONCEPT	
LESSON	
INSTRUCTOR	

THIS CLASS	WAS THE MOST...
	EDUCATIONAL
	WORK
	FUN
	BORING

MAXIMUM POSSIBILITY

1) MOTIVATION	2) INSPIRATION	3) HIGHER EDUCATION	4) CAREER	5) DREAM
6) INVENTION	7) INNOVATION	8) NON-PROFIT	9) FORTUNE 500	10) SUPERHERO

RECORD IT

HOW WAS SCHOOL TODAY?

DATE:_____

HOW DID YOU GET ALONG WITH PEOPLE?

ALLIES: POSITIVE / NEGATIVE / NEUTRAL

ANNOYANCES: POSITIVE / NEGATIVE / NEUTRAL   INSTRUCTORS: POSITIVE / NEGATIVE / NEUTRAL

HOW DID YOU BEHAVE?

SUCCESSES: MAJOR / MINOR / NONE

STRUGGLES: MAJOR / MINOR / NONE

CONFESSIONS: MAJOR / MINOR / NONE

HOW WAS YOUR ENERGY?

MORNING: FULL TANK / HALF TANK / EMPTY   NOON: FULL TANK / HALF TANK / EMPTY

AFTERNOON: FULL TANK / HALF TANK / EMPTY

DID YOU NEED THE NURSE?

HEALTH: YES / NO   INJURY: YES / NO   PAIN: YES / NO

HOW WAS THE FOOD?

BREAKFAST: DELICIOUS / DECENT / DISGUSTING / DIDN'T EAT

LUNCH: DELICIOUS / DECENT / DISGUSTING / DIDN'T EAT

SNACKS: DELICIOUS / DECENT / DISGUSTING / DIDN'T EAT

QUIET   ANNOYED   COOL   SAD   TIRED   EXCITED   HAPPY   EMBARRASSED   SCARED

BORED   SICK   FRUSTRATED   ANGRY   FUNNY   PROUD   NERVOUS   GOOFY   SURPRISED

B = BEST PART OF YOUR DAY   **W** = WORST PART OF YOUR DAY   **M** = MOST OF THE DAY

RECORD IT
WHAT DID YOU LEARN TODAY?

MINIMUM FUNCTIONALITY

1) ABILITY	2) SKILL	3) VOCATION	4) RELATIONSHIP	5) MENTALITY
6) MENTAL EXERCISE	7) MUSCLE MEMORY	8) PRACTICE	9) TRAINING	10) EXPERIENCE

IN THIS CLASS	I ENGAGED MOST BY ...	MINIMUM FUNCTIONALITY	THIS CLASS	MAXIMUM POSSIBILITY
	THINKING SEEING LISTENING DOING			
	THINKING SEEING LISTENING DOING			
	THINKING SEEING LISTENING DOING			
	THINKING SEEING LISTENING DOING			
	THINKING SEEING LISTENING DOING			
	THINKING SEEING LISTENING DOING			
	THINKING SEEING LISTENING DOING			
	THINKING SEEING LISTENING DOING			

THIS INSTRUCTOR	BROUGHT ME THE MOST...
	EDUCATION
	TEACHING
	FUN
	CHALLENGES

THIS...	BROUGHT ME THE MOST ISSUES
CLASS	
CONCEPT	
LESSON	
INSTRUCTOR	

THIS CLASS	WAS THE MOST...
	EDUCATIONAL
	WORK
	FUN
	BORING

MAXIMUM POSSIBILITY

1) MOTIVATION	2) INSPIRATION	3) HIGHER EDUCATION	4) CAREER	5) DREAM
6) INVENTION	7) INNOVATION	8) NON-PROFIT	9) FORTUNE 500	10) SUPERHERO

RECORD IT

HOW WAS SCHOOL TODAY?

DATE:_____

HOW DID YOU GET ALONG WITH PEOPLE?

ALLIES: POSITIVE / NEGATIVE / NEUTRAL

ANNOYANCES: POSITIVE / NEGATIVE / NEUTRAL   INSTRUCTORS: POSITIVE / NEGATIVE / NEUTRAL

HOW DID YOU BEHAVE?

SUCCESSES: MAJOR / MINOR / NONE

STRUGGLES: MAJOR / MINOR / NONE

CONFESSIONS: MAJOR / MINOR / NONE

HOW WAS YOUR ENERGY?

MORNING: FULL TANK / HALF TANK / EMPTY   NOON: FULL TANK / HALF TANK / EMPTY

AFTERNOON: FULL TANK / HALF TANK / EMPTY

DID YOU NEED THE NURSE?

HEALTH: YES / NO   INJURY: YES / NO   PAIN: YES / NO

HOW WAS THE FOOD?

BREAKFAST: DELICIOUS / DECENT / DISGUSTING / DIDN'T EAT

LUNCH: DELICIOUS / DECENT / DISGUSTING / DIDN'T EAT

SNACKS: DELICIOUS / DECENT / DISGUSTING / DIDN'T EAT

QUIET   ANNOYED   COOL   SAD   TIRED   EXCITED   HAPPY   EMBARRASSED   SCARED

BORED   SICK   FRUSTRATED   ANGRY   FUNNY   PROUD   NERVOUS   GOOFY   SURPRISED

B = BEST PART OF YOUR DAY   **W** = WORST PART OF YOUR DAY   **M** = MOST OF THE DAY

RECORD IT
WHAT DID YOU LEARN TODAY?

MINIMUM FUNCTIONALITY

1) ABILITY	2) SKILL	3) VOCATION	4) RELATIONSHIP	5) MENTALITY
6) MENTAL EXERCISE	7) MUSCLE MEMORY	8) PRACTICE	9) TRAINING	10) EXPERIENCE

IN THIS CLASS	I ENGAGED MOST BY ...	MINIMUM FUNCTIONALITY	THIS CLASS	MAXIMUM POSSIBILITY
	THINKING SEEING LISTENING DOING			
	THINKING SEEING LISTENING DOING			
	THINKING SEEING LISTENING DOING			
	THINKING SEEING LISTENING DOING			
	THINKING SEEING LISTENING DOING			
	THINKING SEEING LISTENING DOING			
	THINKING SEEING LISTENING DOING			
	THINKING SEEING LISTENING DOING			

THIS INSTRUCTOR	BROUGHT ME THE MOST...
	EDUCATION
	TEACHING
	FUN
	CHALLENGES

THIS...	BROUGHT ME THE MOST ISSUES
CLASS	
CONCEPT	
LESSON	
INSTRUCTOR	

THIS CLASS	WAS THE MOST...
	EDUCATIONAL
	WORK
	FUN
	BORING

MAXIMUM POSSIBILITY

1) MOTIVATION	2) INSPIRATION	3) HIGHER EDUCATION	4) CAREER	5) DREAM
6) INVENTION	7) INNOVATION	8) NON-PROFIT	9) FORTUNE 500	10) SUPERHERO

RECORD IT
HOW WAS SCHOOL TODAY?

DATE:_____

HOW DID YOU GET ALONG WITH PEOPLE?

ALLIES: POSITIVE / NEGATIVE / NEUTRAL

ANNOYANCES: POSITIVE / NEGATIVE / NEUTRAL   INSTRUCTORS: POSITIVE / NEGATIVE / NEUTRAL

HOW DID YOU BEHAVE?

SUCCESSES: MAJOR / MINOR / NONE

STRUGGLES: MAJOR / MINOR / NONE

CONFESSIONS: MAJOR / MINOR / NONE

HOW WAS YOUR ENERGY?

MORNING: FULL TANK / HALF TANK / EMPTY   NOON: FULL TANK / HALF TANK / EMPTY

AFTERNOON: FULL TANK / HALF TANK / EMPTY

DID YOU NEED THE NURSE?

HEALTH: YES / NO   INJURY: YES / NO   PAIN: YES / NO

HOW WAS THE FOOD?

BREAKFAST: DELICIOUS / DECENT / DISGUSTING / DIDN'T EAT

LUNCH: DELICIOUS / DECENT / DISGUSTING / DIDN'T EAT

SNACKS: DELICIOUS / DECENT / DISGUSTING / DIDN'T EAT

QUIET   ANNOYED   COOL   SAD   TIRED   EXCITED   HAPPY   EMBARRASSED   SCARED

BORED   SICK   FRUSTRATED   ANGRY   FUNNY   PROUD   NERVOUS   GOOFY   SURPRISED

B = BEST PART OF YOUR DAY   **W** = WORST PART OF YOUR DAY   **M** = MOST OF THE DAY

RECORD IT
WHAT DID YOU LEARN TODAY?

MINIMUM FUNCTIONALITY

1) ABILITY	2) SKILL	3) VOCATION	4) RELATIONSHIP	5) MENTALITY
6) MENTAL EXERCISE	7) MUSCLE MEMORY	8) PRACTICE	9) TRAINING	10) EXPERIENCE

IN THIS CLASS	I ENGAGED MOST BY ...	MINIMUM FUNCTIONALITY	THIS CLASS	MAXIMUM POSSIBILITY
	THINKING SEEING LISTENING DOING			
	THINKING SEEING LISTENING DOING			
	THINKING SEEING LISTENING DOING			
	THINKING SEEING LISTENING DOING			
	THINKING SEEING LISTENING DOING			
	THINKING SEEING LISTENING DOING			
	THINKING SEEING LISTENING DOING			
	THINKING SEEING LISTENING DOING			

THIS INSTRUCTOR	BROUGHT ME THE MOST...
	EDUCATION
	TEACHING
	FUN
	CHALLENGES

THIS...	BROUGHT ME THE MOST ISSUES
CLASS	
CONCEPT	
LESSON	
INSTRUCTOR	

THIS CLASS	WAS THE MOST...
	EDUCATIONAL
	WORK
	FUN
	BORING

MAXIMUM POSSIBILITY

1) MOTIVATION	2) INSPIRATION	3) HIGHER EDUCATION	4) CAREER	5) DREAM
6) INVENTION	7) INNOVATION	8) NON-PROFIT	9) FORTUNE 500	10) SUPERHERO

HOW WAS SCHOOL TODAY?

DATE:_____

HOW DID YOU GET ALONG WITH PEOPLE?

ALLIES: POSITIVE / NEGATIVE / NEUTRAL

ANNOYANCES: POSITIVE / NEGATIVE / NEUTRAL   INSTRUCTORS: POSITIVE / NEGATIVE / NEUTRAL

HOW DID YOU BEHAVE?

SUCCESSES: MAJOR / MINOR / NONE

STRUGGLES: MAJOR / MINOR / NONE

CONFESSIONS: MAJOR / MINOR / NONE

HOW WAS YOUR ENERGY?

MORNING: FULL TANK / HALF TANK / EMPTY   NOON: FULL TANK / HALF TANK / EMPTY

AFTERNOON: FULL TANK / HALF TANK / EMPTY

DID YOU NEED THE NURSE?

HEALTH: YES / NO   INJURY: YES / NO   PAIN: YES / NO

HOW WAS THE FOOD?

BREAKFAST: DELICIOUS / DECENT / DISGUSTING / DIDN'T EAT

LUNCH: DELICIOUS / DECENT / DISGUSTING / DIDN'T EAT

SNACKS: DELICIOUS / DECENT / DISGUSTING / DIDN'T EAT

 QUIET
 ANNOYED
 COOL
 SAD
 TIRED
 EXCITED
 HAPPY
 EMBARRASSED
 SCARED

 BORED
 SICK
 FRUSTRATED
 ANGRY
 FUNNY
 PROUD
 NERVOUS
 GOOFY
 SURPRISED

B = BEST PART OF YOUR DAY   W = WORST PART OF YOUR DAY   M = MOST OF THE DAY

RECORD IT
WHAT DID YOU LEARN TODAY?

MINIMUM FUNCTIONALITY

1) ABILITY	2) SKILL	3) VOCATION	4) RELATIONSHIP	5) MENTALITY
6) MENTAL EXERCISE	7) MUSCLE MEMORY	8) PRACTICE	9) TRAINING	10) EXPERIENCE

IN THIS CLASS	I ENGAGED MOST BY ...	MINIMUM FUNCTIONALITY	THIS CLASS	MAXIMUM POSSIBILITY
	THINKING SEEING LISTENING DOING			
	THINKING SEEING LISTENING DOING			
	THINKING SEEING LISTENING DOING			
	THINKING SEEING LISTENING DOING			
	THINKING SEEING LISTENING DOING			
	THINKING SEEING LISTENING DOING			
	THINKING SEEING LISTENING DOING			
	THINKING SEEING LISTENING DOING			

THIS INSTRUCTOR	BROUGHT ME THE MOST...
	EDUCATION
	TEACHING
	FUN
	CHALLENGES

THIS...	BROUGHT ME THE MOST ISSUES
CLASS	
CONCEPT	
LESSON	
INSTRUCTOR	

THIS CLASS	WAS THE MOST...
	EDUCATIONAL
	WORK
	FUN
	BORING

MAXIMUM POSSIBILITY

1) MOTIVATION	2) INSPIRATION	3) HIGHER EDUCATION	4) CAREER	5) DREAM
6) INVENTION	7) INNOVATION	8) NON-PROFIT	9) FORTUNE 500	10) SUPERHERO

How Was School Today?

DATE:_____

HOW DID YOU GET ALONG WITH PEOPLE?

ALLIES: POSITIVE / NEGATIVE / NEUTRAL

ANNOYANCES: POSITIVE / NEGATIVE / NEUTRAL   INSTRUCTORS: POSITIVE / NEGATIVE / NEUTRAL

HOW DID YOU BEHAVE?

SUCCESSES: MAJOR / MINOR / NONE

STRUGGLES: MAJOR / MINOR / NONE

CONFESSIONS: MAJOR / MINOR / NONE

HOW WAS YOUR ENERGY?

MORNING: FULL TANK / HALF TANK / EMPTY   NOON: FULL TANK / HALF TANK / EMPTY

AFTERNOON: FULL TANK / HALF TANK / EMPTY

DID YOU NEED THE NURSE?

HEALTH: YES / NO   INJURY: YES / NO   PAIN: YES / NO

HOW WAS THE FOOD?

BREAKFAST: DELICIOUS / DECENT / DISGUSTING / DIDN'T EAT

LUNCH: DELICIOUS / DECENT / DISGUSTING / DIDN'T EAT

SNACKS: DELICIOUS / DECENT / DISGUSTING / DIDN'T EAT

QUIET   ANNOYED   COOL   SAD   TIRED   EXCITED   HAPPY   EMBARRASSED   SCARED

BORED   SICK   FRUSTRATED   ANGRY   FUNNY   PROUD   NERVOUS   GOOFY   SURPRISED

B = BEST PART OF YOUR DAY   **W** = WORST PART OF YOUR DAY   **M** = MOST OF THE DAY

RECORD IT
WHAT DID YOU LEARN TODAY?

1) ABILITY	2) SKILL	3) VOCATION	4) RELATIONSHIP	5) MENTALITY
6) MENTAL EXERCISE	7) MUSCLE MEMORY	8) PRACTICE	9) TRAINING	10) EXPERIENCE

IN THIS CLASS	I ENGAGED MOST BY ...	MINIMUM FUNCTIONALITY	THIS CLASS	MAXIMUM POSSIBILITY
	THINKING SEEING LISTENING DOING			
	THINKING SEEING LISTENING DOING			
	THINKING SEEING LISTENING DOING			
	THINKING SEEING LISTENING DOING			
	THINKING SEEING LISTENING DOING			
	THINKING SEEING LISTENING DOING			
	THINKING SEEING LISTENING DOING			
	THINKING SEEING LISTENING DOING			

THIS INSTRUCTOR	BROUGHT ME THE MOST...
	EDUCATION
	TEACHING
	FUN
	CHALLENGES

THIS...	BROUGHT ME THE MOST ISSUES
CLASS	
CONCEPT	
LESSON	
INSTRUCTOR	

THIS CLASS	WAS THE MOST...
	EDUCATIONAL
	WORK
	FUN
	BORING

MAXIMUM POSSIBILITY

1) MOTIVATION	2) INSPIRATION	3) HIGHER EDUCATION	4) CAREER	5) DREAM
6) INVENTION	7) INNOVATION	8) NON-PROFIT	9) FORTUNE 500	10) SUPERHERO

RECORD IT

How Was School Today?

DATE:_____

HOW DID YOU GET ALONG WITH PEOPLE?

ALLIES: POSITIVE / NEGATIVE / NEUTRAL

ANNOYANCES: POSITIVE / NEGATIVE / NEUTRAL   INSTRUCTORS: POSITIVE / NEGATIVE / NEUTRAL

HOW DID YOU BEHAVE?

SUCCESSES: MAJOR / MINOR / NONE

STRUGGLES: MAJOR / MINOR / NONE

CONFESSIONS: MAJOR / MINOR / NONE

HOW WAS YOUR ENERGY?

MORNING: FULL TANK / HALF TANK / EMPTY   NOON: FULL TANK / HALF TANK / EMPTY

AFTERNOON: FULL TANK / HALF TANK / EMPTY

DID YOU NEED THE NURSE?

HEALTH: YES / NO   INJURY: YES / NO   PAIN: YES / NO

HOW WAS THE FOOD?

BREAKFAST: DELICIOUS / DECENT / DISGUSTING / DIDN'T EAT

LUNCH: DELICIOUS / DECENT / DISGUSTING / DIDN'T EAT

SNACKS: DELICIOUS / DECENT / DISGUSTING / DIDN'T EAT

 QUIET
 ANNOYED
 COOL
 SAD
 TIRED
 EXCITED
 HAPPY
 EMBARRASSED
 SCARED

 BORED
 SICK
 FRUSTRATED
 ANGRY
 FUNNY
 PROUD
 NERVOUS
 GOOFY
 SURPRISED

B = BEST PART OF YOUR DAY   **W** = WORST PART OF YOUR DAY   **M** = MOST OF THE DAY

RECORD IT
WHAT DID YOU LEARN TODAY?

MINIMUM FUNCTIONALITY

1) ABILITY	2) SKILL	3) VOCATION	4) RELATIONSHIP	5) MENTALITY
6) MENTAL EXERCISE	7) MUSCLE MEMORY	8) PRACTICE	9) TRAINING	10) EXPERIENCE

IN THIS CLASS	I ENGAGED MOST BY...	MINIMUM FUNCTIONALITY	THIS CLASS	MAXIMUM POSSIBILITY
	THINKING SEEING LISTENING DOING			
	THINKING SEEING LISTENING DOING			
	THINKING SEEING LISTENING DOING			
	THINKING SEEING LISTENING DOING			
	THINKING SEEING LISTENING DOING			
	THINKING SEEING LISTENING DOING			
	THINKING SEEING LISTENING DOING			
	THINKING SEEING LISTENING DOING			

THIS INSTRUCTOR	BROUGHT ME THE MOST...
	EDUCATION
	TEACHING
	FUN
	CHALLENGES

THIS...	BROUGHT ME THE MOST ISSUES
CLASS	
CONCEPT	
LESSON	
INSTRUCTOR	

THIS CLASS	WAS THE MOST...
	EDUCATIONAL
	WORK
	FUN
	BORING

MAXIMUM POSSIBILITY

1) MOTIVATION	2) INSPIRATION	3) HIGHER EDUCATION	4) CAREER	5) DREAM
6) INVENTION	7) INNOVATION	8) NON-PROFIT	9) FORTUNE 500	10) SUPERHERO

How Was School Today?

DATE:_____

HOW DID YOU GET ALONG WITH PEOPLE?

ALLIES: POSITIVE / NEGATIVE / NEUTRAL

ANNOYANCES: POSITIVE / NEGATIVE / NEUTRAL   INSTRUCTORS: POSITIVE / NEGATIVE / NEUTRAL

HOW DID YOU BEHAVE?

SUCCESSES: MAJOR / MINOR / NONE

STRUGGLES: MAJOR / MINOR / NONE

CONFESSIONS: MAJOR / MINOR / NONE

HOW WAS YOUR ENERGY?

MORNING: FULL TANK / HALF TANK / EMPTY   NOON: FULL TANK / HALF TANK / EMPTY

AFTERNOON: FULL TANK / HALF TANK / EMPTY

DID YOU NEED THE NURSE?

HEALTH: YES / NO   INJURY: YES / NO   PAIN: YES / NO

HOW WAS THE FOOD?

BREAKFAST: DELICIOUS / DECENT / DISGUSTING / DIDN'T EAT

LUNCH: DELICIOUS / DECENT / DISGUSTING / DIDN'T EAT

SNACKS: DELICIOUS / DECENT / DISGUSTING / DIDN'T EAT

QUIET   ANNOYED   COOL   SAD   TIRED   EXCITED   HAPPY   EMBARRASSED   SCARED

BORED   SICK   FRUSTRATED   ANGRY   FUNNY   PROUD   NERVOUS   GOOFY   SURPRISED

B = BEST PART OF YOUR DAY   W = WORST PART OF YOUR DAY   M = MOST OF THE DAY

RECORD IT
WHAT DID YOU LEARN TODAY?

MINIMUM FUNCTIONALITY

1) ABILITY	2) SKILL	3) VOCATION	4) RELATIONSHIP	5) MENTALITY
6) MENTAL EXERCISE	7) MUSCLE MEMORY	8) PRACTICE	9) TRAINING	10) EXPERIENCE

IN THIS CLASS	I ENGAGED MOST BY ...	MINIMUM FUNCTIONALITY	THIS CLASS	MAXIMUM POSSIBILITY
	THINKING SEEING LISTENING DOING			
	THINKING SEEING LISTENING DOING			
	THINKING SEEING LISTENING DOING			
	THINKING SEEING LISTENING DOING			
	THINKING SEEING LISTENING DOING			
	THINKING SEEING LISTENING DOING			
	THINKING SEEING LISTENING DOING			
	THINKING SEEING LISTENING DOING			

THIS INSTRUCTOR	BROUGHT ME THE MOST...
	EDUCATION
	TEACHING
	FUN
	CHALLENGES

THIS...	BROUGHT ME THE MOST ISSUES
CLASS	
CONCEPT	
LESSON	
INSTRUCTOR	

THIS CLASS	WAS THE MOST...
	EDUCATIONAL
	WORK
	FUN
	BORING

MAXIMUM POSSIBILITY

1) MOTIVATION	2) INSPIRATION	3) HIGHER EDUCATION	4) CAREER	5) DREAM
6) INVENTION	7) INNOVATION	8) NON-PROFIT	9) FORTUNE 500	10) SUPERHERO

RECORD IT
How Was School Today?

DATE: _____

HOW DID YOU GET ALONG WITH PEOPLE?

ALLIES: POSITIVE / NEGATIVE / NEUTRAL

ANNOYANCES: POSITIVE / NEGATIVE / NEUTRAL   INSTRUCTORS: POSITIVE / NEGATIVE / NEUTRAL

HOW DID YOU BEHAVE?

SUCCESSES: MAJOR / MINOR / NONE

STRUGGLES: MAJOR / MINOR / NONE

CONFESSIONS: MAJOR / MINOR / NONE

HOW WAS YOUR ENERGY?

MORNING: FULL TANK / HALF TANK / EMPTY   NOON: FULL TANK / HALF TANK / EMPTY

AFTERNOON: FULL TANK / HALF TANK / EMPTY

DID YOU NEED THE NURSE?

HEALTH: YES / NO   INJURY: YES / NO   PAIN: YES / NO

HOW WAS THE FOOD?

BREAKFAST: DELICIOUS / DECENT / DISGUSTING / DIDN'T EAT

LUNCH: DELICIOUS / DECENT / DISGUSTING / DIDN'T EAT

SNACKS: DELICIOUS / DECENT / DISGUSTING / DIDN'T EAT

QUIET   ANNOYED   COOL   SAD   TIRED   EXCITED   HAPPY   EMBARRASSED   SCARED

BORED   SICK   FRUSTRATED   ANGRY   FUNNY   PROUD   NERVOUS   GOOFY   SURPRISED

B = BEST PART OF YOUR DAY   W = WORST PART OF YOUR DAY   M = MOST OF THE DAY

RECORD IT
WHAT DID YOU LEARN TODAY?

MINIMUM FUNCTIONALITY

1) ABILITY	2) SKILL	3) VOCATION	4) RELATIONSHIP	5) MENTALITY
6) MENTAL EXERCISE	7) MUSCLE MEMORY	8) PRACTICE	9) TRAINING	10) EXPERIENCE

IN THIS CLASS	I ENGAGED MOST BY ...
	THINKING SEEING LISTENING DOING
	THINKING SEEING LISTENING DOING
	THINKING SEEING LISTENING DOING
	THINKING SEEING LISTENING DOING
	THINKING SEEING LISTENING DOING
	THINKING SEEING LISTENING DOING
	THINKING SEEING LISTENING DOING
	THINKING SEEING LISTENING DOING

MINIMUM FUNCTIONALITY	THIS CLASS	MAXIMUM POSSIBILITY

THIS INSTRUCTOR	BROUGHT ME THE MOST...
	EDUCATION
	TEACHING
	FUN
	CHALLENGES

THIS...	BROUGHT ME THE MOST ISSUES
CLASS	
CONCEPT	
LESSON	
INSTRUCTOR	

THIS CLASS	WAS THE MOST...
	EDUCATIONAL
	WORK
	FUN
	BORING

MAXIMUM POSSIBILITY

1) MOTIVATION	2) INSPIRATION	3) HIGHER EDUCATION	4) CAREER	5) DREAM
6) INVENTION	7) INNOVATION	8) NON-PROFIT	9) FORTUNE 500	10) SUPERHERO

RECORD IT

How Was School Today?

DATE:_____

HOW DID YOU GET ALONG WITH PEOPLE?

ALLIES: POSITIVE / NEGATIVE / NEUTRAL

ANNOYANCES: POSITIVE / NEGATIVE / NEUTRAL   INSTRUCTORS: POSITIVE / NEGATIVE / NEUTRAL

HOW DID YOU BEHAVE?

SUCCESSES: MAJOR / MINOR / NONE

STRUGGLES: MAJOR / MINOR / NONE

CONFESSIONS: MAJOR / MINOR / NONE

HOW WAS YOUR ENERGY?

MORNING: FULL TANK / HALF TANK / EMPTY   NOON: FULL TANK / HALF TANK / EMPTY

AFTERNOON: FULL TANK / HALF TANK / EMPTY

DID YOU NEED THE NURSE?

HEALTH: YES / NO   INJURY: YES / NO   PAIN: YES / NO

HOW WAS THE FOOD?

BREAKFAST: DELICIOUS / DECENT / DISGUSTING / DIDN'T EAT

LUNCH: DELICIOUS / DECENT / DISGUSTING / DIDN'T EAT

SNACKS: DELICIOUS / DECENT / DISGUSTING / DIDN'T EAT

QUIET   ANNOYED   COOL   SAD   TIRED   EXCITED   HAPPY   EMBARRASSED   SCARED

BORED   SICK   FRUSTRATED   ANGRY   FUNNY   PROUD   NERVOUS   GOOFY   SURPRISED

B = BEST PART OF YOUR DAY   **W** = WORST PART OF YOUR DAY   **M** = MOST OF THE DAY

RECORD IT
WHAT DID YOU LEARN TODAY?

1) ABILITY	2) SKILL	3) VOCATION	4) RELATIONSHIP	5) MENTALITY
6) MENTAL EXERCISE	7) MUSCLE MEMORY	8) PRACTICE	9) TRAINING	10) EXPERIENCE

IN THIS CLASS	I ENGAGED MOST BY ...	MINIMUM FUNCTIONALITY	THIS CLASS	MAXIMUM POSSIBILITY
	THINKING SEEING LISTENING DOING			
	THINKING SEEING LISTENING DOING			
	THINKING SEEING LISTENING DOING			
	THINKING SEEING LISTENING DOING			
	THINKING SEEING LISTENING DOING			
	THINKING SEEING LISTENING DOING			
	THINKING SEEING LISTENING DOING			
	THINKING SEEING LISTENING DOING			

THIS INSTRUCTOR	BROUGHT ME THE MOST...
	EDUCATION
	TEACHING
	FUN
	CHALLENGES

THIS...	BROUGHT ME THE MOST ISSUES
CLASS	
CONCEPT	
LESSON	
INSTRUCTOR	

THIS CLASS	WAS THE MOST...
	EDUCATIONAL
	WORK
	FUN
	BORING

MAXIMUM POSSIBILITY

1) MOTIVATION	2) INSPIRATION	3) HIGHER EDUCATION	4) CAREER	5) DREAM
6) INVENTION	7) INNOVATION	8) NON-PROFIT	9) FORTUNE 500	10) SUPERHERO

HOW WAS SCHOOL TODAY?

DATE: _____

HOW DID YOU GET ALONG WITH PEOPLE?

ALLIES: POSITIVE / NEGATIVE / NEUTRAL

ANNOYANCES: POSITIVE / NEGATIVE / NEUTRAL   INSTRUCTORS: POSITIVE / NEGATIVE / NEUTRAL

HOW DID YOU BEHAVE?

SUCCESSES: MAJOR / MINOR / NONE

STRUGGLES: MAJOR / MINOR / NONE

CONFESSIONS: MAJOR / MINOR / NONE

HOW WAS YOUR ENERGY?

MORNING: FULL TANK / HALF TANK / EMPTY   NOON: FULL TANK / HALF TANK / EMPTY

AFTERNOON: FULL TANK / HALF TANK / EMPTY

DID YOU NEED THE NURSE?

HEALTH: YES / NO   INJURY: YES / NO   PAIN: YES / NO

HOW WAS THE FOOD?

BREAKFAST: DELICIOUS / DECENT / DISGUSTING / DIDN'T EAT

LUNCH: DELICIOUS / DECENT / DISGUSTING / DIDN'T EAT

SNACKS: DELICIOUS / DECENT / DISGUSTING / DIDN'T EAT

QUIET   ANNOYED   COOL   SAD   TIRED   EXCITED   HAPPY   EMBARRASSED   SCARED

BORED   SICK   FRUSTRATED   ANGRY   FUNNY   PROUD   NERVOUS   GOOFY   SURPRISED

B = BEST PART OF YOUR DAY   **W** = WORST PART OF YOUR DAY   **M** = MOST OF THE DAY

RECORD IT
WHAT DID YOU LEARN TODAY?

MINIMUM FUNCTIONALITY

1) ABILITY	2) SKILL	3) VOCATION	4) RELATIONSHIP	5) MENTALITY
6) MENTAL EXERCISE	7) MUSCLE MEMORY	8) PRACTICE	9) TRAINING	10) EXPERIENCE

IN THIS CLASS	I ENGAGED MOST BY ...	MINIMUM FUNCTIONALITY	THIS CLASS	MAXIMUM POSSIBILITY
	THINKING SEEING LISTENING DOING			
	THINKING SEEING LISTENING DOING			
	THINKING SEEING LISTENING DOING			
	THINKING SEEING LISTENING DOING			
	THINKING SEEING LISTENING DOING			
	THINKING SEEING LISTENING DOING			
	THINKING SEEING LISTENING DOING			
	THINKING SEEING LISTENING DOING			

THIS INSTRUCTOR	BROUGHT ME THE MOST...
	EDUCATION
	TEACHING
	FUN
	CHALLENGES

THIS...	BROUGHT ME THE MOST ISSUES
CLASS	
CONCEPT	
LESSON	
INSTRUCTOR	

THIS CLASS	WAS THE MOST...
	EDUCATIONAL
	WORK
	FUN
	BORING

MAXIMUM POSSIBILITY

1) MOTIVATION	2) INSPIRATION	3) HIGHER EDUCATION	4) CAREER	5) DREAM
6) INVENTION	7) INNOVATION	8) NON-PROFIT	9) FORTUNE 500	10) SUPERHERO

RECORD IT
HOW WAS SCHOOL TODAY?

DATE:_____

HOW DID YOU GET ALONG WITH PEOPLE?

ALLIES: POSITIVE / NEGATIVE / NEUTRAL

ANNOYANCES: POSITIVE / NEGATIVE / NEUTRAL   INSTRUCTORS: POSITIVE / NEGATIVE / NEUTRAL

HOW DID YOU BEHAVE?

SUCCESSES: MAJOR / MINOR / NONE

STRUGGLES: MAJOR / MINOR / NONE

CONFESSIONS: MAJOR / MINOR / NONE

HOW WAS YOUR ENERGY?

MORNING: FULL TANK / HALF TANK / EMPTY   NOON: FULL TANK / HALF TANK / EMPTY

AFTERNOON: FULL TANK / HALF TANK / EMPTY

DID YOU NEED THE NURSE?

HEALTH: YES / NO   INJURY: YES / NO   PAIN: YES / NO

HOW WAS THE FOOD?

BREAKFAST: DELICIOUS / DECENT / DISGUSTING / DIDN'T EAT

LUNCH: DELICIOUS / DECENT / DISGUSTING / DIDN'T EAT

SNACKS: DELICIOUS / DECENT / DISGUSTING / DIDN'T EAT

QUIET   ANNOYED   COOL   SAD   TIRED   EXCITED   HAPPY   EMBARRASSED   SCARED

BORED   SICK   FRUSTRATED   ANGRY   FUNNY   PROUD   NERVOUS   GOOFY   SURPRISED

B = BEST PART OF YOUR DAY   **W** = WORST PART OF YOUR DAY   **M** = MOST OF THE DAY

RECORD IT
WHAT DID YOU LEARN TODAY?

MINIMUM FUNCTIONALITY

1) ABILITY	2) SKILL	3) VOCATION	4) RELATIONSHIP	5) MENTALITY
6) MENTAL EXERCISE	7) MUSCLE MEMORY	8) PRACTICE	9) TRAINING	10) EXPERIENCE

IN THIS CLASS	I ENGAGED MOST BY …	MINIMUM FUNCTIONALITY	THIS CLASS	MAXIMUM POSSIBILITY
	THINKING SEEING LISTENING DOING			
	THINKING SEEING LISTENING DOING			
	THINKING SEEING LISTENING DOING			
	THINKING SEEING LISTENING DOING			
	THINKING SEEING LISTENING DOING			
	THINKING SEEING LISTENING DOING			
	THINKING SEEING LISTENING DOING			
	THINKING SEEING LISTENING DOING			

THIS INSTRUCTOR	BROUGHT ME THE MOST…
	EDUCATION
	TEACHING
	FUN
	CHALLENGES

THIS…	BROUGHT ME THE MOST ISSUES
CLASS	
CONCEPT	
LESSON	
INSTRUCTOR	

THIS CLASS	WAS THE MOST…
	EDUCATIONAL
	WORK
	FUN
	BORING

MAXIMUM POSSIBILITY

1) MOTIVATION	2) INSPIRATION	3) HIGHER EDUCATION	4) CAREER	5) DREAM
6) INVENTION	7) INNOVATION	8) NON-PROFIT	9) FORTUNE 500	10) SUPERHERO

RECORD IT

HOW WAS SCHOOL TODAY?

DATE:_____

HOW DID YOU GET ALONG WITH PEOPLE?

ALLIES: POSITIVE / NEGATIVE / NEUTRAL

ANNOYANCES: POSITIVE / NEGATIVE / NEUTRAL   INSTRUCTORS: POSITIVE / NEGATIVE / NEUTRAL

HOW DID YOU BEHAVE?

SUCCESSES: MAJOR / MINOR / NONE

STRUGGLES: MAJOR / MINOR / NONE

CONFESSIONS: MAJOR / MINOR / NONE

HOW WAS YOUR ENERGY?

MORNING: FULL TANK / HALF TANK / EMPTY   NOON: FULL TANK / HALF TANK / EMPTY

AFTERNOON: FULL TANK / HALF TANK / EMPTY

DID YOU NEED THE NURSE?

HEALTH: YES / NO   INJURY: YES / NO   PAIN: YES / NO

HOW WAS THE FOOD?

BREAKFAST: DELICIOUS / DECENT / DISGUSTING / DIDN'T EAT

LUNCH: DELICIOUS / DECENT / DISGUSTING / DIDN'T EAT

SNACKS: DELICIOUS / DECENT / DISGUSTING / DIDN'T EAT

QUIET   ANNOYED   COOL   SAD   TIRED   EXCITED   HAPPY   EMBARRASSED   SCARED

BORED   SICK   FRUSTRATED   ANGRY   FUNNY   PROUD   NERVOUS   GOOFY   SURPRISED

B = BEST PART OF YOUR DAY   **W** = WORST PART OF YOUR DAY   **M** = MOST OF THE DAY

RECORD IT
WHAT DID YOU LEARN TODAY?

MINIMUM FUNCTIONALITY

1) ABILITY	2) SKILL	3) VOCATION	4) RELATIONSHIP	5) MENTALITY
6) MENTAL EXERCISE	7) MUSCLE MEMORY	8) PRACTICE	9) TRAINING	10) EXPERIENCE

IN THIS CLASS	I ENGAGED MOST BY ...	MINIMUM FUNCTIONALITY	THIS CLASS	MAXIMUM POSSIBILITY
	THINKING SEEING LISTENING DOING			
	THINKING SEEING LISTENING DOING			
	THINKING SEEING LISTENING DOING			
	THINKING SEEING LISTENING DOING			
	THINKING SEEING LISTENING DOING			
	THINKING SEEING LISTENING DOING			
	THINKING SEEING LISTENING DOING			
	THINKING SEEING LISTENING DOING			

THIS INSTRUCTOR	BROUGHT ME THE MOST...
	EDUCATION
	TEACHING
	FUN
	CHALLENGES

THIS...	BROUGHT ME THE MOST ISSUES
CLASS	
CONCEPT	
LESSON	
INSTRUCTOR	

THIS CLASS	WAS THE MOST...
	EDUCATIONAL
	WORK
	FUN
	BORING

MAXIMUM POSSIBILITY

1) MOTIVATION	2) INSPIRATION	3) HIGHER EDUCATION	4) CAREER	5) DREAM
6) INVENTION	7) INNOVATION	8) NON-PROFIT	9) FORTUNE 500	10) SUPERHERO

RECORD IT
How Was School Today?

DATE:_____

HOW DID YOU GET ALONG WITH PEOPLE?

ALLIES: POSITIVE / NEGATIVE / NEUTRAL

ANNOYANCES: POSITIVE / NEGATIVE / NEUTRAL   INSTRUCTORS: POSITIVE / NEGATIVE / NEUTRAL

HOW DID YOU BEHAVE?

SUCCESSES: MAJOR / MINOR / NONE

STRUGGLES: MAJOR / MINOR / NONE

CONFESSIONS: MAJOR / MINOR / NONE

HOW WAS YOUR ENERGY?

MORNING: FULL TANK / HALF TANK / EMPTY   NOON: FULL TANK / HALF TANK / EMPTY

AFTERNOON: FULL TANK / HALF TANK / EMPTY

DID YOU NEED THE NURSE?

HEALTH: YES / NO   INJURY: YES / NO   PAIN: YES / NO

HOW WAS THE FOOD?

BREAKFAST: DELICIOUS / DECENT / DISGUSTING / DIDN'T EAT

LUNCH: DELICIOUS / DECENT / DISGUSTING / DIDN'T EAT

SNACKS: DELICIOUS / DECENT / DISGUSTING / DIDN'T EAT

 QUIET
 ANNOYED
 COOL
 SAD
 TIRED
 EXCITED
 HAPPY
 EMBARRASSED
 SCARED

 BORED
 SICK
 FRUSTRATED
 ANGRY
 FUNNY
 PROUD
 NERVOUS
 GOOFY
SURPRISED

B = BEST PART OF YOUR DAY   W = WORST PART OF YOUR DAY   M = MOST OF THE DAY

RECORD IT
WHAT DID YOU LEARN TODAY?

MINIMUM FUNCTIONALITY

1) ABILITY	2) SKILL	3) VOCATION	4) RELATIONSHIP	5) MENTALITY
6) MENTAL EXERCISE	7) MUSCLE MEMORY	8) PRACTICE	9) TRAINING	10) EXPERIENCE

IN THIS CLASS	I ENGAGED MOST BY ...	MINIMUM FUNCTIONALITY	THIS CLASS	MAXIMUM POSSIBILITY
	THINKING SEEING LISTENING DOING			
	THINKING SEEING LISTENING DOING			
	THINKING SEEING LISTENING DOING			
	THINKING SEEING LISTENING DOING			
	THINKING SEEING LISTENING DOING			
	THINKING SEEING LISTENING DOING			
	THINKING SEEING LISTENING DOING			
	THINKING SEEING LISTENING DOING			

THIS INSTRUCTOR	BROUGHT ME THE MOST...
	EDUCATION
	TEACHING
	FUN
	CHALLENGES

THIS...	BROUGHT ME THE MOST ISSUES
CLASS	
CONCEPT	
LESSON	
INSTRUCTOR	

THIS CLASS	WAS THE MOST...
	EDUCATIONAL
	WORK
	FUN
	BORING

MAXIMUM POSSIBILITY

1) MOTIVATION	2) INSPIRATION	3) HIGHER EDUCATION	4) CAREER	5) DREAM
6) INVENTION	7) INNOVATION	8) NON-PROFIT	9) FORTUNE 500	10) SUPERHERO

RECORD IT

HOW WAS SCHOOL TODAY?

DATE:_____

HOW DID YOU GET ALONG WITH PEOPLE?

ALLIES: POSITIVE / NEGATIVE / NEUTRAL

ANNOYANCES: POSITIVE / NEGATIVE / NEUTRAL   INSTRUCTORS: POSITIVE / NEGATIVE / NEUTRAL

HOW DID YOU BEHAVE?

SUCCESSES: MAJOR / MINOR / NONE

STRUGGLES: MAJOR / MINOR / NONE

CONFESSIONS: MAJOR / MINOR / NONE

HOW WAS YOUR ENERGY?

MORNING: FULL TANK / HALF TANK / EMPTY   NOON: FULL TANK / HALF TANK / EMPTY

AFTERNOON: FULL TANK / HALF TANK / EMPTY

DID YOU NEED THE NURSE?

HEALTH: YES / NO   INJURY: YES / NO   PAIN: YES / NO

HOW WAS THE FOOD?

BREAKFAST: DELICIOUS / DECENT / DISGUSTING / DIDN'T EAT

LUNCH: DELICIOUS / DECENT / DISGUSTING / DIDN'T EAT

SNACKS: DELICIOUS / DECENT / DISGUSTING / DIDN'T EAT

QUIET   ANNOYED   COOL   SAD   TIRED   EXCITED   HAPPY   EMBARRASSED   SCARED

BORED   SICK   FRUSTRATED   ANGRY   FUNNY   PROUD   NERVOUS   GOOFY   SURPRISED

B = BEST PART OF YOUR DAY   W = WORST PART OF YOUR DAY   M = MOST OF THE DAY

RECORD IT
WHAT DID YOU LEARN TODAY?

MINIMUM FUNCTIONALITY

1) ABILITY	2) SKILL	3) VOCATION	4) RELATIONSHIP	5) MENTALITY
6) MENTAL EXERCISE	7) MUSCLE MEMORY	8) PRACTICE	9) TRAINING	10) EXPERIENCE

IN THIS CLASS	I ENGAGED MOST BY ...
	THINKING SEEING LISTENING DOING
	THINKING SEEING LISTENING DOING
	THINKING SEEING LISTENING DOING
	THINKING SEEING LISTENING DOING
	THINKING SEEING LISTENING DOING
	THINKING SEEING LISTENING DOING
	THINKING SEEING LISTENING DOING
	THINKING SEEING LISTENING DOING

MINIMUM FUNCTIONALITY	THIS CLASS	MAXIMUM POSSIBILITY

THIS INSTRUCTOR	BROUGHT ME THE MOST...
	EDUCATION
	TEACHING
	FUN
	CHALLENGES

THIS...	BROUGHT ME THE MOST ISSUES
CLASS	
CONCEPT	
LESSON	
INSTRUCTOR	

THIS CLASS	WAS THE MOST...
	EDUCATIONAL
	WORK
	FUN
	BORING

MAXIMUM POSSIBILITY

1) MOTIVATION	2) INSPIRATION	3) HIGHER EDUCATION	4) CAREER	5) DREAM
6) INVENTION	7) INNOVATION	8) NON-PROFIT	9) FORTUNE 500	10) SUPERHERO

RECORD IT
How Was School Today?

DATE: _____

HOW DID YOU GET ALONG WITH PEOPLE?

ALLIES: POSITIVE / NEGATIVE / NEUTRAL

ANNOYANCES: POSITIVE / NEGATIVE / NEUTRAL   INSTRUCTORS: POSITIVE / NEGATIVE / NEUTRAL

HOW DID YOU BEHAVE?

SUCCESSES: MAJOR / MINOR / NONE

STRUGGLES: MAJOR / MINOR / NONE

CONFESSIONS: MAJOR / MINOR / NONE

HOW WAS YOUR ENERGY?

MORNING: FULL TANK / HALF TANK / EMPTY   NOON: FULL TANK / HALF TANK / EMPTY

AFTERNOON: FULL TANK / HALF TANK / EMPTY

DID YOU NEED THE NURSE?

HEALTH: YES / NO   INJURY: YES / NO   PAIN: YES / NO

HOW WAS THE FOOD?

BREAKFAST: DELICIOUS / DECENT / DISGUSTING / DIDN'T EAT

LUNCH: DELICIOUS / DECENT / DISGUSTING / DIDN'T EAT

SNACKS: DELICIOUS / DECENT / DISGUSTING / DIDN'T EAT

QUIET   ANNOYED   COOL   SAD   TIRED   EXCITED   HAPPY   EMBARRASSED   SCARED

BORED   SICK   FRUSTRATED   ANGRY   FUNNY   PROUD   NERVOUS   GOOFY   SURPRISED

B = BEST PART OF YOUR DAY   **W** = WORST PART OF YOUR DAY   **M** = MOST OF THE DAY

RECORD IT
WHAT DID YOU LEARN TODAY?

1) ABILITY	2) SKILL	3) VOCATION	4) RELATIONSHIP	5) MENTALITY
6) MENTAL EXERCISE	7) MUSCLE MEMORY	8) PRACTICE	9) TRAINING	10) EXPERIENCE

IN THIS CLASS	I ENGAGED MOST BY ...	MINIMUM FUNCTIONALITY	THIS CLASS	MAXIMUM POSSIBILITY
	THINKING SEEING LISTENING DOING			
	THINKING SEEING LISTENING DOING			
	THINKING SEEING LISTENING DOING			
	THINKING SEEING LISTENING DOING			
	THINKING SEEING LISTENING DOING			
	THINKING SEEING LISTENING DOING			
	THINKING SEEING LISTENING DOING			
	THINKING SEEING LISTENING DOING			

THIS INSTRUCTOR	BROUGHT ME THE MOST...
	EDUCATION
	TEACHING
	FUN
	CHALLENGES

THIS...	BROUGHT ME THE MOST ISSUES
CLASS	
CONCEPT	
LESSON	
INSTRUCTOR	

THIS CLASS	WAS THE MOST...
	EDUCATIONAL
	WORK
	FUN
	BORING

MAXIMUM POSSIBILITY

1) MOTIVATION	2) INSPIRATION	3) HIGHER EDUCATION	4) CAREER	5) DREAM
6) INVENTION	7) INNOVATION	8) NON-PROFIT	9) FORTUNE 500	10) SUPERHERO

HOW WAS SCHOOL TODAY?

DATE:_____

HOW DID YOU GET ALONG WITH PEOPLE?

ALLIES: POSITIVE / NEGATIVE / NEUTRAL

ANNOYANCES: POSITIVE / NEGATIVE / NEUTRAL   INSTRUCTORS: POSITIVE / NEGATIVE / NEUTRAL

HOW DID YOU BEHAVE?

SUCCESSES: MAJOR / MINOR / NONE

STRUGGLES: MAJOR / MINOR / NONE

CONFESSIONS: MAJOR / MINOR / NONE

HOW WAS YOUR ENERGY?

MORNING: FULL TANK / HALF TANK / EMPTY   NOON: FULL TANK / HALF TANK / EMPTY

AFTERNOON: FULL TANK / HALF TANK / EMPTY

DID YOU NEED THE NURSE?

HEALTH: YES / NO   INJURY: YES / NO   PAIN: YES / NO

HOW WAS THE FOOD?

BREAKFAST: DELICIOUS / DECENT / DISGUSTING / DIDN'T EAT

LUNCH: DELICIOUS / DECENT / DISGUSTING / DIDN'T EAT

SNACKS: DELICIOUS / DECENT / DISGUSTING / DIDN'T EAT

QUIET   ANNOYED   COOL   SAD   TIRED   EXCITED   HAPPY   EMBARRASSED   SCARED

BORED   SICK   FRUSTRATED   ANGRY   FUNNY   PROUD   NERVOUS   GOOFY   SURPRISED

B = BEST PART OF YOUR DAY   **W** = WORST PART OF YOUR DAY   **M** = MOST OF THE DAY

RECORD IT
WHAT DID YOU LEARN TODAY?

MINIMUM FUNCTIONALITY

1) ABILITY	2) SKILL	3) VOCATION	4) RELATIONSHIP	5) MENTALITY
6) MENTAL EXERCISE	7) MUSCLE MEMORY	8) PRACTICE	9) TRAINING	10) EXPERIENCE

IN THIS CLASS	I ENGAGED MOST BY ...	MINIMUM FUNCTIONALITY	THIS CLASS	MAXIMUM POSSIBILITY
	THINKING SEEING LISTENING DOING			
	THINKING SEEING LISTENING DOING			
	THINKING SEEING LISTENING DOING			
	THINKING SEEING LISTENING DOING			
	THINKING SEEING LISTENING DOING			
	THINKING SEEING LISTENING DOING			
	THINKING SEEING LISTENING DOING			
	THINKING SEEING LISTENING DOING			

THIS INSTRUCTOR	BROUGHT ME THE MOST...
	EDUCATION
	TEACHING
	FUN
	CHALLENGES

THIS...	BROUGHT ME THE MOST ISSUES
CLASS	
CONCEPT	
LESSON	
INSTRUCTOR	

THIS CLASS	WAS THE MOST...
	EDUCATIONAL
	WORK
	FUN
	BORING

MAXIMUM POSSIBILITY

1) MOTIVATION	2) INSPIRATION	3) HIGHER EDUCATION	4) CAREER	5) DREAM
6) INVENTION	7) INNOVATION	8) NON-PROFIT	9) FORTUNE 500	10) SUPERHERO

RECORD IT

How Was School Today?

DATE: _____

HOW DID YOU GET ALONG WITH PEOPLE?

ALLIES: POSITIVE / NEGATIVE / NEUTRAL

ANNOYANCES: POSITIVE / NEGATIVE / NEUTRAL   INSTRUCTORS: POSITIVE / NEGATIVE / NEUTRAL

HOW DID YOU BEHAVE?

SUCCESSES: MAJOR / MINOR / NONE

STRUGGLES: MAJOR / MINOR / NONE

CONFESSIONS: MAJOR / MINOR / NONE

HOW WAS YOUR ENERGY?

MORNING: FULL TANK / HALF TANK / EMPTY   NOON: FULL TANK / HALF TANK / EMPTY

AFTERNOON: FULL TANK / HALF TANK / EMPTY

DID YOU NEED THE NURSE?

HEALTH: YES / NO   INJURY: YES / NO   PAIN: YES / NO

HOW WAS THE FOOD?

BREAKFAST: DELICIOUS / DECENT / DISGUSTING / DIDN'T EAT

LUNCH: DELICIOUS / DECENT / DISGUSTING / DIDN'T EAT

SNACKS: DELICIOUS / DECENT / DISGUSTING / DIDN'T EAT

 QUIET
 ANNOYED
 COOL
 SAD
 TIRED
 EXCITED
 HAPPY
 EMBARRASSED
 SCARED

 BORED
 SICK
 FRUSTRATED
 ANGRY

 FUNNY
 PROUD
 NERVOUS
 GOOFY
 SURPRISED

B = BEST PART OF YOUR DAY   **W** = WORST PART OF YOUR DAY   **M** = MOST OF THE DAY

RECORD IT
WHAT DID YOU LEARN TODAY?

MINIMUM FUNCTIONALITY

1) ABILITY	2) SKILL	3) VOCATION	4) RELATIONSHIP	5) MENTALITY
6) MENTAL EXERCISE	7) MUSCLE MEMORY	8) PRACTICE	9) TRAINING	10) EXPERIENCE

IN THIS CLASS	I ENGAGED MOST BY ...	MINIMUM FUNCTIONALITY	THIS CLASS	MAXIMUM POSSIBILITY
	THINKING SEEING LISTENING DOING			
	THINKING SEEING LISTENING DOING			
	THINKING SEEING LISTENING DOING			
	THINKING SEEING LISTENING DOING			
	THINKING SEEING LISTENING DOING			
	THINKING SEEING LISTENING DOING			
	THINKING SEEING LISTENING DOING			
	THINKING SEEING LISTENING DOING			

THIS INSTRUCTOR	BROUGHT ME THE MOST...
	EDUCATION
	TEACHING
	FUN
	CHALLENGES

THIS...	BROUGHT ME THE MOST ISSUES
CLASS	
CONCEPT	
LESSON	
INSTRUCTOR	

THIS CLASS	WAS THE MOST...
	EDUCATIONAL
	WORK
	FUN
	BORING

MAXIMUM POSSIBILITY

1) MOTIVATION	2) INSPIRATION	3) HIGHER EDUCATION	4) CAREER	5) DREAM
6) INVENTION	7) INNOVATION	8) NON-PROFIT	9) FORTUNE 500	10) SUPERHERO

HOW WAS SCHOOL TODAY?

DATE:_____

HOW DID YOU GET ALONG WITH PEOPLE?

ALLIES: POSITIVE / NEGATIVE / NEUTRAL

ANNOYANCES: POSITIVE / NEGATIVE / NEUTRAL   INSTRUCTORS: POSITIVE / NEGATIVE / NEUTRAL

HOW DID YOU BEHAVE?

SUCCESSES: MAJOR / MINOR / NONE

STRUGGLES: MAJOR / MINOR / NONE

CONFESSIONS: MAJOR / MINOR / NONE

HOW WAS YOUR ENERGY?

MORNING: FULL TANK / HALF TANK / EMPTY   NOON: FULL TANK / HALF TANK / EMPTY

AFTERNOON: FULL TANK / HALF TANK / EMPTY

DID YOU NEED THE NURSE?

HEALTH: YES / NO   INJURY: YES / NO   PAIN: YES / NO

HOW WAS THE FOOD?

BREAKFAST: DELICIOUS / DECENT / DISGUSTING / DIDN'T EAT

LUNCH: DELICIOUS / DECENT / DISGUSTING / DIDN'T EAT

SNACKS: DELICIOUS / DECENT / DISGUSTING / DIDN'T EAT

QUIET   ANNOYED   COOL   SAD   TIRED   EXCITED   HAPPY   EMBARRASSED   SCARED

BORED   SICK   FRUSTRATED   ANGRY   FUNNY   PROUD   NERVOUS   GOOFY   SURPRISED

B = BEST PART OF YOUR DAY   **W** = WORST PART OF YOUR DAY   **M** = MOST OF THE DAY

RECORD IT
WHAT DID YOU LEARN TODAY?

MINIMUM FUNCTIONALITY

1) ABILITY	2) SKILL	3) VOCATION	4) RELATIONSHIP	5) MENTALITY
6) MENTAL EXERCISE	7) MUSCLE MEMORY	8) PRACTICE	9) TRAINING	10) EXPERIENCE

IN THIS CLASS	I ENGAGED MOST BY ...	MINIMUM FUNCTIONALITY	THIS CLASS	MAXIMUM POSSIBILITY
	THINKING SEEING LISTENING DOING			
	THINKING SEEING LISTENING DOING			
	THINKING SEEING LISTENING DOING			
	THINKING SEEING LISTENING DOING			
	THINKING SEEING LISTENING DOING			
	THINKING SEEING LISTENING DOING			
	THINKING SEEING LISTENING DOING			
	THINKING SEEING LISTENING DOING			

THIS INSTRUCTOR	BROUGHT ME THE MOST...
	EDUCATION
	TEACHING
	FUN
	CHALLENGES

THIS...	BROUGHT ME THE MOST ISSUES
CLASS	
CONCEPT	
LESSON	
INSTRUCTOR	

THIS CLASS	WAS THE MOST...
	EDUCATIONAL
	WORK
	FUN
	BORING

MAXIMUM POSSIBILITY

1) MOTIVATION	2) INSPIRATION	3) HIGHER EDUCATION	4) CAREER	5) DREAM
6) INVENTION	7) INNOVATION	8) NON-PROFIT	9) FORTUNE 500	10) SUPERHERO

RECORD IT
How Was School Today?

DATE: _____

HOW DID YOU GET ALONG WITH PEOPLE?

ALLIES: POSITIVE / NEGATIVE / NEUTRAL

ANNOYANCES: POSITIVE / NEGATIVE / NEUTRAL   INSTRUCTORS: POSITIVE / NEGATIVE / NEUTRAL

HOW DID YOU BEHAVE?

SUCCESSES: MAJOR / MINOR / NONE

STRUGGLES: MAJOR / MINOR / NONE

CONFESSIONS: MAJOR / MINOR / NONE

HOW WAS YOUR ENERGY?

MORNING: FULL TANK / HALF TANK / EMPTY   NOON: FULL TANK / HALF TANK / EMPTY

AFTERNOON: FULL TANK / HALF TANK / EMPTY

DID YOU NEED THE NURSE?

HEALTH: YES / NO   INJURY: YES / NO   PAIN: YES / NO

HOW WAS THE FOOD?

BREAKFAST: DELICIOUS / DECENT / DISGUSTING / DIDN'T EAT

LUNCH: DELICIOUS / DECENT / DISGUSTING / DIDN'T EAT

SNACKS: DELICIOUS / DECENT / DISGUSTING / DIDN'T EAT

QUIET   ANNOYED   COOL   SAD   TIRED   EXCITED   HAPPY   EMBARRASSED   SCARED

BORED   SICK   FRUSTRATED   ANGRY   FUNNY   PROUD   NERVOUS   GOOFY   SURPRISED

B = BEST PART OF YOUR DAY   W = WORST PART OF YOUR DAY   M = MOST OF THE DAY

RECORD IT
WHAT DID YOU LEARN TODAY?

MINIMUM FUNCTIONALITY

1) ABILITY	2) SKILL	3) VOCATION	4) RELATIONSHIP	5) MENTALITY
6) MENTAL EXERCISE	7) MUSCLE MEMORY	8) PRACTICE	9) TRAINING	10) EXPERIENCE

IN THIS CLASS	I ENGAGED MOST BY ...
	THINKING SEEING LISTENING DOING
	THINKING SEEING LISTENING DOING
	THINKING SEEING LISTENING DOING
	THINKING SEEING LISTENING DOING
	THINKING SEEING LISTENING DOING
	THINKING SEEING LISTENING DOING
	THINKING SEEING LISTENING DOING
	THINKING SEEING LISTENING DOING

MINIMUM FUNCTIONALITY	THIS CLASS	MAXIMUM POSSIBILITY

THIS INSTRUCTOR	BROUGHT ME THE MOST...
	EDUCATION
	TEACHING
	FUN
	CHALLENGES

THIS...	BROUGHT ME THE MOST ISSUES
CLASS	
CONCEPT	
LESSON	
INSTRUCTOR	

THIS CLASS	WAS THE MOST...
	EDUCATIONAL
	WORK
	FUN
	BORING

MAXIMUM POSSIBILITY

1) MOTIVATION	2) INSPIRATION	3) HIGHER EDUCATION	4) CAREER	5) DREAM
6) INVENTION	7) INNOVATION	8) NON-PROFIT	9) FORTUNE 500	10) SUPERHERO

RECORD IT
HOW WAS SCHOOL TODAY?

DATE:_____

HOW DID YOU GET ALONG WITH PEOPLE?

ALLIES: POSITIVE / NEGATIVE / NEUTRAL

ANNOYANCES: POSITIVE / NEGATIVE / NEUTRAL   INSTRUCTORS: POSITIVE / NEGATIVE / NEUTRAL

HOW DID YOU BEHAVE?

SUCCESSES: MAJOR / MINOR / NONE

STRUGGLES: MAJOR / MINOR / NONE

CONFESSIONS: MAJOR / MINOR / NONE

HOW WAS YOUR ENERGY?

MORNING: FULL TANK / HALF TANK / EMPTY   NOON: FULL TANK / HALF TANK / EMPTY

AFTERNOON: FULL TANK / HALF TANK / EMPTY

DID YOU NEED THE NURSE?

HEALTH: YES / NO   INJURY: YES / NO   PAIN: YES / NO

HOW WAS THE FOOD?

BREAKFAST: DELICIOUS / DECENT / DISGUSTING / DIDN'T EAT

LUNCH: DELICIOUS / DECENT / DISGUSTING / DIDN'T EAT

SNACKS: DELICIOUS / DECENT / DISGUSTING / DIDN'T EAT

QUIET   ANNOYED   COOL   SAD   TIRED   EXCITED   HAPPY   EMBARRASSED   SCARED

BORED   SICK   FRUSTRATED   ANGRY   FUNNY   PROUD   NERVOUS   GOOFY   SURPRISED

B = BEST PART OF YOUR DAY   **W** = WORST PART OF YOUR DAY   **M** = MOST OF THE DAY

RECORD IT
WHAT DID YOU LEARN TODAY?

MINIMUM FUNCTIONALITY

1) ABILITY	2) SKILL	3) VOCATION	4) RELATIONSHIP	5) MENTALITY
6) MENTAL EXERCISE	7) MUSCLE MEMORY	8) PRACTICE	9) TRAINING	10) EXPERIENCE

IN THIS CLASS	I ENGAGED MOST BY ...	MINIMUM FUNCTIONALITY	THIS CLASS	MAXIMUM POSSIBILITY
	THINKING SEEING LISTENING DOING			
	THINKING SEEING LISTENING DOING			
	THINKING SEEING LISTENING DOING			
	THINKING SEEING LISTENING DOING			
	THINKING SEEING LISTENING DOING			
	THINKING SEEING LISTENING DOING			
	THINKING SEEING LISTENING DOING			
	THINKING SEEING LISTENING DOING			

THIS INSTRUCTOR	BROUGHT ME THE MOST...
	EDUCATION
	TEACHING
	FUN
	CHALLENGES

THIS...	BROUGHT ME THE MOST ISSUES
CLASS	
CONCEPT	
LESSON	
INSTRUCTOR	

THIS CLASS	WAS THE MOST...
	EDUCATIONAL
	WORK
	FUN
	BORING

MAXIMUM POSSIBILITY

1) MOTIVATION	2) INSPIRATION	3) HIGHER EDUCATION	4) CAREER	5) DREAM
6) INVENTION	7) INNOVATION	8) NON-PROFIT	9) FORTUNE 500	10) SUPERHERO

RECORD IT

HOW WAS SCHOOL TODAY?

DATE:_____

HOW DID YOU GET ALONG WITH PEOPLE?

ALLIES: POSITIVE / NEGATIVE / NEUTRAL

ANNOYANCES: POSITIVE / NEGATIVE / NEUTRAL   INSTRUCTORS: POSITIVE / NEGATIVE / NEUTRAL

HOW DID YOU BEHAVE?

SUCCESSES: MAJOR / MINOR / NONE

STRUGGLES: MAJOR / MINOR / NONE

CONFESSIONS: MAJOR / MINOR / NONE

HOW WAS YOUR ENERGY?

MORNING: FULL TANK / HALF TANK / EMPTY   NOON: FULL TANK / HALF TANK / EMPTY

AFTERNOON: FULL TANK / HALF TANK / EMPTY

DID YOU NEED THE NURSE?

HEALTH: YES / NO   INJURY: YES / NO   PAIN: YES / NO

HOW WAS THE FOOD?

BREAKFAST: DELICIOUS / DECENT / DISGUSTING / DIDN'T EAT

LUNCH: DELICIOUS / DECENT / DISGUSTING / DIDN'T EAT

SNACKS: DELICIOUS / DECENT / DISGUSTING / DIDN'T EAT

QUIET   ANNOYED   COOL   SAD   TIRED   EXCITED   HAPPY   EMBARRASSED   SCARED

BORED   SICK   FRUSTRATED   ANGRY   FUNNY   PROUD   NERVOUS   GOOFY   SURPRISED

B = BEST PART OF YOUR DAY   **W** = WORST PART OF YOUR DAY   **M** = MOST OF THE DAY

RECORD IT
WHAT DID YOU LEARN TODAY?

1) ABILITY	2) SKILL	3) VOCATION	4) RELATIONSHIP	5) MENTALITY
6) MENTAL EXERCISE	7) MUSCLE MEMORY	8) PRACTICE	9) TRAINING	10) EXPERIENCE

IN THIS CLASS	I ENGAGED MOST BY ...	MINIMUM FUNCTIONALITY	THIS CLASS	MAXIMUM POSSIBILITY
	THINKING SEEING LISTENING DOING			
	THINKING SEEING LISTENING DOING			
	THINKING SEEING LISTENING DOING			
	THINKING SEEING LISTENING DOING			
	THINKING SEEING LISTENING DOING			
	THINKING SEEING LISTENING DOING			
	THINKING SEEING LISTENING DOING			
	THINKING SEEING LISTENING DOING			

THIS INSTRUCTOR	BROUGHT ME THE MOST...
	EDUCATION
	TEACHING
	FUN
	CHALLENGES

THIS...	BROUGHT ME THE MOST ISSUES
CLASS	
CONCEPT	
LESSON	
INSTRUCTOR	

THIS CLASS	WAS THE MOST...
	EDUCATIONAL
	WORK
	FUN
	BORING

MAXIMUM POSSIBILITY

1) MOTIVATION	2) INSPIRATION	3) HIGHER EDUCATION	4) CAREER	5) DREAM
6) INVENTION	7) INNOVATION	8) NON-PROFIT	9) FORTUNE 500	10) SUPERHERO

RECORD IT
HOW WAS SCHOOL TODAY?

DATE:_____

HOW DID YOU GET ALONG WITH PEOPLE?

ALLIES: POSITIVE / NEGATIVE / NEUTRAL

ANNOYANCES: POSITIVE / NEGATIVE / NEUTRAL   INSTRUCTORS: POSITIVE / NEGATIVE / NEUTRAL

HOW DID YOU BEHAVE?

SUCCESSES: MAJOR / MINOR / NONE

STRUGGLES: MAJOR / MINOR / NONE

CONFESSIONS: MAJOR / MINOR / NONE

HOW WAS YOUR ENERGY?

MORNING: FULL TANK / HALF TANK / EMPTY   NOON: FULL TANK / HALF TANK / EMPTY

AFTERNOON: FULL TANK / HALF TANK / EMPTY

DID YOU NEED THE NURSE?

HEALTH: YES / NO   INJURY: YES / NO   PAIN: YES / NO

HOW WAS THE FOOD?

BREAKFAST: DELICIOUS / DECENT / DISGUSTING / DIDN'T EAT

LUNCH: DELICIOUS / DECENT / DISGUSTING / DIDN'T EAT

SNACKS: DELICIOUS / DECENT / DISGUSTING / DIDN'T EAT

QUIET   ANNOYED   COOL   SAD   TIRED   EXCITED   HAPPY   EMBARRASSED   SCARED

BORED   SICK   FRUSTRATED   ANGRY   FUNNY   PROUD   NERVOUS   GOOFY   SURPRISED

B = BEST PART OF YOUR DAY   **W** = WORST PART OF YOUR DAY   **M** = MOST OF THE DAY

RECORD IT
WHAT DID YOU LEARN TODAY?

MINIMUM FUNCTIONALITY

1) ABILITY	2) SKILL	3) VOCATION	4) RELATIONSHIP	5) MENTALITY
6) MENTAL EXERCISE	7) MUSCLE MEMORY	8) PRACTICE	9) TRAINING	10) EXPERIENCE

IN THIS CLASS	I ENGAGED MOST BY ...
	THINKING SEEING LISTENING DOING
	THINKING SEEING LISTENING DOING
	THINKING SEEING LISTENING DOING
	THINKING SEEING LISTENING DOING
	THINKING SEEING LISTENING DOING
	THINKING SEEING LISTENING DOING
	THINKING SEEING LISTENING DOING
	THINKING SEEING LISTENING DOING

MINIMUM FUNCTIONALITY	THIS CLASS	MAXIMUM POSSIBILITY

THIS INSTRUCTOR	BROUGHT ME THE MOST...
	EDUCATION
	TEACHING
	FUN
	CHALLENGES

THIS...	BROUGHT ME THE MOST ISSUES
CLASS	
CONCEPT	
LESSON	
INSTRUCTOR	

THIS CLASS	WAS THE MOST...
	EDUCATIONAL
	WORK
	FUN
	BORING

MAXIMUM POSSIBILITY

1) MOTIVATION	2) INSPIRATION	3) HIGHER EDUCATION	4) CAREER	5) DREAM
6) INVENTION	7) INNOVATION	8) NON-PROFIT	9) FORTUNE 500	10) SUPERHERO

RECORD IT

How Was School Today?

DATE: _____

HOW DID YOU GET ALONG WITH PEOPLE?

ALLIES: POSITIVE / NEGATIVE / NEUTRAL

ANNOYANCES: POSITIVE / NEGATIVE / NEUTRAL   INSTRUCTORS: POSITIVE / NEGATIVE / NEUTRAL

HOW DID YOU BEHAVE?

SUCCESSES: MAJOR / MINOR / NONE

STRUGGLES: MAJOR / MINOR / NONE

CONFESSIONS: MAJOR / MINOR / NONE

HOW WAS YOUR ENERGY?

MORNING: FULL TANK / HALF TANK / EMPTY   NOON: FULL TANK / HALF TANK / EMPTY

AFTERNOON: FULL TANK / HALF TANK / EMPTY

DID YOU NEED THE NURSE?

HEALTH: YES / NO   INJURY: YES / NO   PAIN: YES / NO

HOW WAS THE FOOD?

BREAKFAST: DELICIOUS / DECENT / DISGUSTING / DIDN'T EAT

LUNCH: DELICIOUS / DECENT / DISGUSTING / DIDN'T EAT

SNACKS: DELICIOUS / DECENT / DISGUSTING / DIDN'T EAT

 QUIET
 ANNOYED
 COOL
 SAD
 TIRED
 EXCITED
 HAPPY
 EMBARRASSED
 SCARED

 BORED
 SICK
 FRUSTRATED
 ANGRY
 FUNNY
 PROUD
 NERVOUS
 GOOFY
 SURPRISED

B = BEST PART OF YOUR DAY   **W** = WORST PART OF YOUR DAY   **M** = MOST OF THE DAY

RECORD IT
WHAT DID YOU LEARN TODAY?

MINIMUM FUNCTIONALITY

| 1) ABILITY | 2) SKILL | 3) VOCATION | 4) RELATIONSHIP | 5) MENTALITY |
| 6) MENTAL EXERCISE | 7) MUSCLE MEMORY | 8) PRACTICE | 9) TRAINING | 10) EXPERIENCE |

IN THIS CLASS	I ENGAGED MOST BY ...	MINIMUM FUNCTIONALITY	THIS CLASS	MAXIMUM POSSIBILITY
	THINKING SEEING LISTENING DOING			
	THINKING SEEING LISTENING DOING			
	THINKING SEEING LISTENING DOING			
	THINKING SEEING LISTENING DOING			
	THINKING SEEING LISTENING DOING			
	THINKING SEEING LISTENING DOING			
	THINKING SEEING LISTENING DOING			
	THINKING SEEING LISTENING DOING			

THIS INSTRUCTOR	BROUGHT ME THE MOST...
	EDUCATION
	TEACHING
	FUN
	CHALLENGES

THIS...	BROUGHT ME THE MOST ISSUES
CLASS	
CONCEPT	
LESSON	
INSTRUCTOR	

THIS CLASS	WAS THE MOST...
	EDUCATIONAL
	WORK
	FUN
	BORING

MAXIMUM POSSIBILITY

| 1) MOTIVATION | 2) INSPIRATION | 3) HIGHER EDUCATION | 4) CAREER | 5) DREAM |
| 6) INVENTION | 7) INNOVATION | 8) NON-PROFIT | 9) FORTUNE 500 | 10) SUPERHERO |

RECORD IT

HOW WAS SCHOOL TODAY?

DATE:_____

HOW DID YOU GET ALONG WITH PEOPLE?

ALLIES: POSITIVE / NEGATIVE / NEUTRAL

ANNOYANCES: POSITIVE / NEGATIVE / NEUTRAL   INSTRUCTORS: POSITIVE / NEGATIVE / NEUTRAL

HOW DID YOU BEHAVE?

SUCCESSES: MAJOR / MINOR / NONE

STRUGGLES: MAJOR / MINOR / NONE

CONFESSIONS: MAJOR / MINOR / NONE

HOW WAS YOUR ENERGY?

MORNING: FULL TANK / HALF TANK / EMPTY   NOON: FULL TANK / HALF TANK / EMPTY

AFTERNOON: FULL TANK / HALF TANK / EMPTY

DID YOU NEED THE NURSE?

HEALTH: YES / NO   INJURY: YES / NO   PAIN: YES / NO

HOW WAS THE FOOD?

BREAKFAST: DELICIOUS / DECENT / DISGUSTING / DIDN'T EAT

LUNCH: DELICIOUS / DECENT / DISGUSTING / DIDN'T EAT

SNACKS: DELICIOUS / DECENT / DISGUSTING / DIDN'T EAT

 QUIET
 ANNOYED
 COOL
 SAD
 TIRED
 EXCITED
 HAPPY
 EMBARRASSED
 SCARED

 BORED
 SICK
 FRUSTRATED
 ANGRY
 FUNNY
 PROUD
 NERVOUS
 GOOFY
 SURPRISED

B = BEST PART OF YOUR DAY   **W** = WORST PART OF YOUR DAY   **M** = MOST OF THE DAY

RECORD IT
WHAT DID YOU LEARN TODAY?

MINIMUM FUNCTIONALITY

| 1) ABILITY | 2) SKILL | 3) VOCATION | 4) RELATIONSHIP | 5) MENTALITY |
| 6) MENTAL EXERCISE | 7) MUSCLE MEMORY | 8) PRACTICE | 9) TRAINING | 10) EXPERIENCE |

IN THIS CLASS	I ENGAGED MOST BY ...	MINIMUM FUNCTIONALITY	THIS CLASS	MAXIMUM POSSIBILITY
	THINKING SEEING LISTENING DOING			
	THINKING SEEING LISTENING DOING			
	THINKING SEEING LISTENING DOING			
	THINKING SEEING LISTENING DOING			
	THINKING SEEING LISTENING DOING			
	THINKING SEEING LISTENING DOING			
	THINKING SEEING LISTENING DOING			
	THINKING SEEING LISTENING DOING			

THIS INSTRUCTOR	BROUGHT ME THE MOST...
	EDUCATION
	TEACHING
	FUN
	CHALLENGES

THIS...	BROUGHT ME THE MOST ISSUES
CLASS	
CONCEPT	
LESSON	
INSTRUCTOR	

THIS CLASS	WAS THE MOST...
	EDUCATIONAL
	WORK
	FUN
	BORING

MAXIMUM POSSIBILITY

| 1) MOTIVATION | 2) INSPIRATION | 3) HIGHER EDUCATION | 4) CAREER | 5) DREAM |
| 6) INVENTION | 7) INNOVATION | 8) NON-PROFIT | 9) FORTUNE 500 | 10) SUPERHERO |

How Was School Today?

DATE:_____

HOW DID YOU GET ALONG WITH PEOPLE?

ALLIES: POSITIVE / NEGATIVE / NEUTRAL

ANNOYANCES: POSITIVE / NEGATIVE / NEUTRAL   INSTRUCTORS: POSITIVE / NEGATIVE / NEUTRAL

HOW DID YOU BEHAVE?

SUCCESSES: MAJOR / MINOR / NONE

STRUGGLES: MAJOR / MINOR / NONE

CONFESSIONS: MAJOR / MINOR / NONE

HOW WAS YOUR ENERGY?

MORNING: FULL TANK / HALF TANK / EMPTY   NOON: FULL TANK / HALF TANK / EMPTY

AFTERNOON: FULL TANK / HALF TANK / EMPTY

DID YOU NEED THE NURSE?

HEALTH: YES / NO   INJURY: YES / NO   PAIN: YES / NO

HOW WAS THE FOOD?

BREAKFAST: DELICIOUS / DECENT / DISGUSTING / DIDN'T EAT

LUNCH: DELICIOUS / DECENT / DISGUSTING / DIDN'T EAT

SNACKS: DELICIOUS / DECENT / DISGUSTING / DIDN'T EAT

QUIET   ANNOYED   COOL   SAD   TIRED   EXCITED   HAPPY   EMBARRASSED   SCARED

BORED   SICK   FRUSTRATED   ANGRY   FUNNY   PROUD   NERVOUS   GOOFY   SURPRISED

B = BEST PART OF YOUR DAY   W = WORST PART OF YOUR DAY   M = MOST OF THE DAY

RECORD IT
WHAT DID YOU LEARN TODAY?

1) ABILITY	2) SKILL	3) VOCATION	4) RELATIONSHIP	5) MENTALITY
6) MENTAL EXERCISE	7) MUSCLE MEMORY	8) PRACTICE	9) TRAINING	10) EXPERIENCE

IN THIS CLASS	I ENGAGED MOST BY ...	MINIMUM FUNCTIONALITY	THIS CLASS	MAXIMUM POSSIBILITY
	THINKING SEEING LISTENING DOING			
	THINKING SEEING LISTENING DOING			
	THINKING SEEING LISTENING DOING			
	THINKING SEEING LISTENING DOING			
	THINKING SEEING LISTENING DOING			
	THINKING SEEING LISTENING DOING			
	THINKING SEEING LISTENING DOING			
	THINKING SEEING LISTENING DOING			

THIS INSTRUCTOR	BROUGHT ME THE MOST...
	EDUCATION
	TEACHING
	FUN
	CHALLENGES

THIS...	BROUGHT ME THE MOST ISSUES
CLASS	
CONCEPT	
LESSON	
INSTRUCTOR	

THIS CLASS	WAS THE MOST...
	EDUCATIONAL
	WORK
	FUN
	BORING

MAXIMUM POSSIBILITY

1) MOTIVATION	2) INSPIRATION	3) HIGHER EDUCATION	4) CAREER	5) DREAM
6) INVENTION	7) INNOVATION	8) NON-PROFIT	9) FORTUNE 500	10) SUPERHERO

RECORD IT

HOW WAS SCHOOL TODAY?

DATE:_____

HOW DID YOU GET ALONG WITH PEOPLE?

ALLIES: POSITIVE / NEGATIVE / NEUTRAL

ANNOYANCES: POSITIVE / NEGATIVE / NEUTRAL   INSTRUCTORS: POSITIVE / NEGATIVE / NEUTRAL

HOW DID YOU BEHAVE?

SUCCESSES: MAJOR / MINOR / NONE

STRUGGLES: MAJOR / MINOR / NONE

CONFESSIONS: MAJOR / MINOR / NONE

HOW WAS YOUR ENERGY?

MORNING: FULL TANK / HALF TANK / EMPTY   NOON: FULL TANK / HALF TANK / EMPTY

AFTERNOON: FULL TANK / HALF TANK / EMPTY

DID YOU NEED THE NURSE?

HEALTH: YES / NO   INJURY: YES / NO   PAIN: YES / NO

HOW WAS THE FOOD?

BREAKFAST: DELICIOUS / DECENT / DISGUSTING / DIDN'T EAT

LUNCH: DELICIOUS / DECENT / DISGUSTING / DIDN'T EAT

SNACKS: DELICIOUS / DECENT / DISGUSTING / DIDN'T EAT

 QUIET
 ANNOYED
 COOL
 SAD
TIRED
EXCITED
 HAPPY
 EMBARRASSED
 SCARED

BORED
 SICK
 FRUSTRATED
 ANGRY
FUNNY
 PROUD
NERVOUS
GOOFY
 SURPRISED

 **B** = BEST PART OF YOUR DAY    **W** = WORST PART OF YOUR DAY    **M** = MOST OF THE DAY

RECORD IT
WHAT DID YOU LEARN TODAY?

MINIMUM FUNCTIONALITY

1) ABILITY	2) SKILL	3) VOCATION	4) RELATIONSHIP	5) MENTALITY
6) MENTAL EXERCISE	7) MUSCLE MEMORY	8) PRACTICE	9) TRAINING	10) EXPERIENCE

IN THIS CLASS	I ENGAGED MOST BY ...	MINIMUM FUNCTIONALITY	THIS CLASS	MAXIMUM POSSIBILITY
	THINKING SEEING LISTENING DOING			
	THINKING SEEING LISTENING DOING			
	THINKING SEEING LISTENING DOING			
	THINKING SEEING LISTENING DOING			
	THINKING SEEING LISTENING DOING			
	THINKING SEEING LISTENING DOING			
	THINKING SEEING LISTENING DOING			
	THINKING SEEING LISTENING DOING			

THIS INSTRUCTOR	BROUGHT ME THE MOST...
	EDUCATION
	TEACHING
	FUN
	CHALLENGES

THIS...	BROUGHT ME THE MOST ISSUES
CLASS	
CONCEPT	
LESSON	
INSTRUCTOR	

THIS CLASS	WAS THE MOST...
	EDUCATIONAL
	WORK
	FUN
	BORING

MAXIMUM POSSIBILITY

1) MOTIVATION	2) INSPIRATION	3) HIGHER EDUCATION	4) CAREER	5) DREAM
6) INVENTION	7) INNOVATION	8) NON-PROFIT	9) FORTUNE 500	10) SUPERHERO

RECORD IT

HOW WAS SCHOOL TODAY?

DATE: _____

HOW DID YOU GET ALONG WITH PEOPLE?

ALLIES: POSITIVE / NEGATIVE / NEUTRAL

ANNOYANCES: POSITIVE / NEGATIVE / NEUTRAL   INSTRUCTORS: POSITIVE / NEGATIVE / NEUTRAL

HOW DID YOU BEHAVE?

SUCCESSES: MAJOR / MINOR / NONE

STRUGGLES: MAJOR / MINOR / NONE

CONFESSIONS: MAJOR / MINOR / NONE

HOW WAS YOUR ENERGY?

MORNING: FULL TANK / HALF TANK / EMPTY   NOON: FULL TANK / HALF TANK / EMPTY

AFTERNOON: FULL TANK / HALF TANK / EMPTY

DID YOU NEED THE NURSE?

HEALTH: YES / NO   INJURY: YES / NO   PAIN: YES / NO

HOW WAS THE FOOD?

BREAKFAST: DELICIOUS / DECENT / DISGUSTING / DIDN'T EAT

LUNCH: DELICIOUS / DECENT / DISGUSTING / DIDN'T EAT

SNACKS: DELICIOUS / DECENT / DISGUSTING / DIDN'T EAT

QUIET   ANNOYED   COOL   SAD   TIRED   EXCITED   HAPPY   EMBARRASSED   SCARED

BORED   SICK   FRUSTRATED   ANGRY   FUNNY   PROUD   NERVOUS   GOOFY   SURPRISED

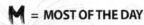

B = BEST PART OF YOUR DAY   **W** = WORST PART OF YOUR DAY   **M** = MOST OF THE DAY

RECORD IT
WHAT DID YOU LEARN TODAY?

MINIMUM FUNCTIONALITY

1) ABILITY	2) SKILL	3) VOCATION	4) RELATIONSHIP	5) MENTALITY
6) MENTAL EXERCISE	7) MUSCLE MEMORY	8) PRACTICE	9) TRAINING	10) EXPERIENCE

IN THIS CLASS	I ENGAGED MOST BY ...	MINIMUM FUNCTIONALITY	THIS CLASS	MAXIMUM POSSIBILITY
	THINKING SEEING LISTENING DOING			
	THINKING SEEING LISTENING DOING			
	THINKING SEEING LISTENING DOING			
	THINKING SEEING LISTENING DOING			
	THINKING SEEING LISTENING DOING			
	THINKING SEEING LISTENING DOING			
	THINKING SEEING LISTENING DOING			
	THINKING SEEING LISTENING DOING			

THIS INSTRUCTOR	BROUGHT ME THE MOST...
	EDUCATION
	TEACHING
	FUN
	CHALLENGES

THIS...	BROUGHT ME THE MOST ISSUES
CLASS	
CONCEPT	
LESSON	
INSTRUCTOR	

THIS CLASS	WAS THE MOST...
	EDUCATIONAL
	WORK
	FUN
	BORING

MAXIMUM POSSIBILITY

1) MOTIVATION	2) INSPIRATION	3) HIGHER EDUCATION	4) CAREER	5) DREAM
6) INVENTION	7) INNOVATION	8) NON-PROFIT	9) FORTUNE 500	10) SUPERHERO

RECORD IT
How Was School Today?

DATE:_____

HOW DID YOU GET ALONG WITH PEOPLE?

ALLIES: POSITIVE / NEGATIVE / NEUTRAL

ANNOYANCES: POSITIVE / NEGATIVE / NEUTRAL   INSTRUCTORS: POSITIVE / NEGATIVE / NEUTRAL

HOW DID YOU BEHAVE?

SUCCESSES: MAJOR / MINOR / NONE

STRUGGLES: MAJOR / MINOR / NONE

CONFESSIONS: MAJOR / MINOR / NONE

HOW WAS YOUR ENERGY?

MORNING: FULL TANK / HALF TANK / EMPTY   NOON: FULL TANK / HALF TANK / EMPTY

AFTERNOON: FULL TANK / HALF TANK / EMPTY

DID YOU NEED THE NURSE?

HEALTH: YES / NO   INJURY: YES / NO   PAIN: YES / NO

HOW WAS THE FOOD?

BREAKFAST: DELICIOUS / DECENT / DISGUSTING / DIDN'T EAT

LUNCH: DELICIOUS / DECENT / DISGUSTING / DIDN'T EAT

SNACKS: DELICIOUS / DECENT / DISGUSTING / DIDN'T EAT

 QUIET
 ANNOYED
 COOL
 SAD
 TIRED
 EXCITED
 HAPPY
EMBARRASSED
SCARED

 BORED
SICK
FRUSTRATED
 ANGRY
 FUNNY
 PROUD
NERVOUS
 GOOFY
 SURPRISED

B = BEST PART OF YOUR DAY   **W** = WORST PART OF YOUR DAY   **M** = MOST OF THE DAY

RECORD IT
WHAT DID YOU LEARN TODAY?

MINIMUM FUNCTIONALITY

1) ABILITY	2) SKILL	3) VOCATION	4) RELATIONSHIP	5) MENTALITY
6) MENTAL EXERCISE	7) MUSCLE MEMORY	8) PRACTICE	9) TRAINING	10) EXPERIENCE

IN THIS CLASS	I ENGAGED MOST BY ...	MINIMUM FUNCTIONALITY	THIS CLASS	MAXIMUM POSSIBILITY
	THINKING SEEING LISTENING DOING			
	THINKING SEEING LISTENING DOING			
	THINKING SEEING LISTENING DOING			
	THINKING SEEING LISTENING DOING			
	THINKING SEEING LISTENING DOING			
	THINKING SEEING LISTENING DOING			
	THINKING SEEING LISTENING DOING			
	THINKING SEEING LISTENING DOING			

THIS INSTRUCTOR	BROUGHT ME THE MOST...
	EDUCATION
	TEACHING
	FUN
	CHALLENGES

THIS...	BROUGHT ME THE MOST ISSUES
CLASS	
CONCEPT	
LESSON	
INSTRUCTOR	

THIS CLASS	WAS THE MOST...
	EDUCATIONAL
	WORK
	FUN
	BORING

MAXIMUM POSSIBILITY

1) MOTIVATION	2) INSPIRATION	3) HIGHER EDUCATION	4) CAREER	5) DREAM
6) INVENTION	7) INNOVATION	8) NON-PROFIT	9) FORTUNE 500	10) SUPERHERO

RECORD IT
How Was School Today?

DATE:_____

HOW DID YOU GET ALONG WITH PEOPLE?

ALLIES: POSITIVE / NEGATIVE / NEUTRAL

ANNOYANCES: POSITIVE / NEGATIVE / NEUTRAL   INSTRUCTORS: POSITIVE / NEGATIVE / NEUTRAL

HOW DID YOU BEHAVE?

SUCCESSES: MAJOR / MINOR / NONE

STRUGGLES: MAJOR / MINOR / NONE

CONFESSIONS: MAJOR / MINOR / NONE

HOW WAS YOUR ENERGY?

MORNING: FULL TANK / HALF TANK / EMPTY   NOON: FULL TANK / HALF TANK / EMPTY

AFTERNOON: FULL TANK / HALF TANK / EMPTY

DID YOU NEED THE NURSE?

HEALTH: YES / NO   INJURY: YES / NO   PAIN: YES / NO

HOW WAS THE FOOD?

BREAKFAST: DELICIOUS / DECENT / DISGUSTING / DIDN'T EAT

LUNCH: DELICIOUS / DECENT / DISGUSTING / DIDN'T EAT

SNACKS: DELICIOUS / DECENT / DISGUSTING / DIDN'T EAT

QUIET   ANNOYED   COOL   SAD   TIRED   EXCITED   HAPPY   EMBARRASSED   SCARED

BORED   SICK   FRUSTRATED   ANGRY   FUNNY   PROUD   NERVOUS   GOOFY   SURPRISED

B = BEST PART OF YOUR DAY   **W** = WORST PART OF YOUR DAY   **M** = MOST OF THE DAY

RECORD IT
WHAT DID YOU LEARN TODAY?

MINIMUM FUNCTIONALITY

1) ABILITY	2) SKILL	3) VOCATION	4) RELATIONSHIP	5) MENTALITY
6) MENTAL EXERCISE	7) MUSCLE MEMORY	8) PRACTICE	9) TRAINING	10) EXPERIENCE

IN THIS CLASS	I ENGAGED MOST BY ...	MINIMUM FUNCTIONALITY	THIS CLASS	MAXIMUM POSSIBILITY
	THINKING SEEING LISTENING DOING			
	THINKING SEEING LISTENING DOING			
	THINKING SEEING LISTENING DOING			
	THINKING SEEING LISTENING DOING			
	THINKING SEEING LISTENING DOING			
	THINKING SEEING LISTENING DOING			
	THINKING SEEING LISTENING DOING			
	THINKING SEEING LISTENING DOING			

THIS INSTRUCTOR	BROUGHT ME THE MOST...
	EDUCATION
	TEACHING
	FUN
	CHALLENGES

THIS...	BROUGHT ME THE MOST ISSUES
CLASS	
CONCEPT	
LESSON	
INSTRUCTOR	

THIS CLASS	WAS THE MOST...
	EDUCATIONAL
	WORK
	FUN
	BORING

MAXIMUM POSSIBILITY

1) MOTIVATION	2) INSPIRATION	3) HIGHER EDUCATION	4) CAREER	5) DREAM
6) INVENTION	7) INNOVATION	8) NON-PROFIT	9) FORTUNE 500	10) SUPERHERO

RECORD IT

HOW WAS SCHOOL TODAY?

DATE:_____

HOW DID YOU GET ALONG WITH PEOPLE?

ALLIES: POSITIVE / NEGATIVE / NEUTRAL

ANNOYANCES: POSITIVE / NEGATIVE / NEUTRAL   INSTRUCTORS: POSITIVE / NEGATIVE / NEUTRAL

HOW DID YOU BEHAVE?

SUCCESSES: MAJOR / MINOR / NONE

STRUGGLES: MAJOR / MINOR / NONE

CONFESSIONS: MAJOR / MINOR / NONE

HOW WAS YOUR ENERGY?

MORNING: FULL TANK / HALF TANK / EMPTY   NOON: FULL TANK / HALF TANK / EMPTY

AFTERNOON: FULL TANK / HALF TANK / EMPTY

DID YOU NEED THE NURSE?

HEALTH: YES / NO   INJURY: YES / NO   PAIN: YES / NO

HOW WAS THE FOOD?

BREAKFAST: DELICIOUS / DECENT / DISGUSTING / DIDN'T EAT

LUNCH: DELICIOUS / DECENT / DISGUSTING / DIDN'T EAT

SNACKS: DELICIOUS / DECENT / DISGUSTING / DIDN'T EAT

QUIET   ANNOYED   COOL   SAD   TIRED   EXCITED   HAPPY   EMBARRASSED   SCARED

BORED   SICK   FRUSTRATED   ANGRY   FUNNY   PROUD   NERVOUS   GOOFY   SURPRISED

  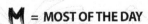

B = BEST PART OF YOUR DAY   **W** = WORST PART OF YOUR DAY   **M** = MOST OF THE DAY

RECORD IT
WHAT DID YOU LEARN TODAY?

MINIMUM FUNCTIONALITY

1) ABILITY	2) SKILL	3) VOCATION	4) RELATIONSHIP	5) MENTALITY
6) MENTAL EXERCISE	7) MUSCLE MEMORY	8) PRACTICE	9) TRAINING	10) EXPERIENCE

IN THIS CLASS	I ENGAGED MOST BY ...	MINIMUM FUNCTIONALITY	THIS CLASS	MAXIMUM POSSIBILITY
	THINKING SEEING LISTENING DOING			
	THINKING SEEING LISTENING DOING			
	THINKING SEEING LISTENING DOING			
	THINKING SEEING LISTENING DOING			
	THINKING SEEING LISTENING DOING			
	THINKING SEEING LISTENING DOING			
	THINKING SEEING LISTENING DOING			
	THINKING SEEING LISTENING DOING			

THIS INSTRUCTOR	BROUGHT ME THE MOST...
	EDUCATION
	TEACHING
	FUN
	CHALLENGES

THIS...	BROUGHT ME THE MOST ISSUES
CLASS	
CONCEPT	
LESSON	
INSTRUCTOR	

THIS CLASS	WAS THE MOST...
	EDUCATIONAL
	WORK
	FUN
	BORING

MAXIMUM POSSIBILITY

1) MOTIVATION	2) INSPIRATION	3) HIGHER EDUCATION	4) CAREER	5) DREAM
6) INVENTION	7) INNOVATION	8) NON-PROFIT	9) FORTUNE 500	10) SUPERHERO

RECORD IT
How Was School Today?

DATE:_____

HOW DID YOU GET ALONG WITH PEOPLE?

ALLIES: POSITIVE / NEGATIVE / NEUTRAL

ANNOYANCES: POSITIVE / NEGATIVE / NEUTRAL   INSTRUCTORS: POSITIVE / NEGATIVE / NEUTRAL

HOW DID YOU BEHAVE?

SUCCESSES: MAJOR / MINOR / NONE

STRUGGLES: MAJOR / MINOR / NONE

CONFESSIONS: MAJOR / MINOR / NONE

HOW WAS YOUR ENERGY?

MORNING: FULL TANK / HALF TANK / EMPTY   NOON: FULL TANK / HALF TANK / EMPTY

AFTERNOON: FULL TANK / HALF TANK / EMPTY

DID YOU NEED THE NURSE?

HEALTH: YES / NO   INJURY: YES / NO   PAIN: YES / NO

HOW WAS THE FOOD?

BREAKFAST: DELICIOUS / DECENT / DISGUSTING / DIDN'T EAT

LUNCH: DELICIOUS / DECENT / DISGUSTING / DIDN'T EAT

SNACKS: DELICIOUS / DECENT / DISGUSTING / DIDN'T EAT

 QUIET
 ANNOYED
 COOL
 SAD
 TIRED
 EXCITED
 HAPPY
 EMBARRASSED
 SCARED

 BORED
 SICK
 FRUSTRATED
 ANGRY
 FUNNY
 PROUD
 NERVOUS
 GOOFY
 SURPRISED

B = BEST PART OF YOUR DAY   **W** = WORST PART OF YOUR DAY   **M** = MOST OF THE DAY

RECORD IT
WHAT DID YOU LEARN TODAY?

<u>MINIMUM FUNCTIONALITY</u>

1) ABILITY	2) SKILL	3) VOCATION	4) RELATIONSHIP	5) MENTALITY
6) MENTAL EXERCISE	7) MUSCLE MEMORY	8) PRACTICE	9) TRAINING	10) EXPERIENCE

IN THIS CLASS	I ENGAGED MOST BY ...	<u>MINIMUM FUNCTIONALITY</u>	**THIS CLASS**	<u>MAXIMUM POSSIBILITY</u>
	THINKING SEEING LISTENING DOING			
	THINKING SEEING LISTENING DOING			
	THINKING SEEING LISTENING DOING			
	THINKING SEEING LISTENING DOING			
	THINKING SEEING LISTENING DOING			
	THINKING SEEING LISTENING DOING			
	THINKING SEEING LISTENING DOING			
	THINKING SEEING LISTENING DOING			

THIS INSTRUCTOR	BROUGHT ME THE MOST...
	EDUCATION
	TEACHING
	FUN
	CHALLENGES

THIS...	BROUGHT ME THE MOST ISSUES
CLASS	
CONCEPT	
LESSON	
INSTRUCTOR	

THIS CLASS	WAS THE MOST...
	EDUCATIONAL
	WORK
	FUN
	BORING

<u>MAXIMUM POSSIBILITY</u>

1) MOTIVATION	2) INSPIRATION	3) HIGHER EDUCATION	4) CAREER	5) DREAM
6) INVENTION	7) INNOVATION	8) NON-PROFIT	9) FORTUNE 500	10) SUPERHERO

RECORD IT

How Was School Today?

DATE:_____

HOW DID YOU GET ALONG WITH PEOPLE?

ALLIES: POSITIVE / NEGATIVE / NEUTRAL

ANNOYANCES: POSITIVE / NEGATIVE / NEUTRAL   INSTRUCTORS: POSITIVE / NEGATIVE / NEUTRAL

HOW DID YOU BEHAVE?

SUCCESSES: MAJOR / MINOR / NONE

STRUGGLES: MAJOR / MINOR / NONE

CONFESSIONS: MAJOR / MINOR / NONE

HOW WAS YOUR ENERGY?

MORNING: FULL TANK / HALF TANK / EMPTY   NOON: FULL TANK / HALF TANK / EMPTY

AFTERNOON: FULL TANK / HALF TANK / EMPTY

DID YOU NEED THE NURSE?

HEALTH: YES / NO   INJURY: YES / NO   PAIN: YES / NO

HOW WAS THE FOOD?

BREAKFAST: DELICIOUS / DECENT / DISGUSTING / DIDN'T EAT

LUNCH: DELICIOUS / DECENT / DISGUSTING / DIDN'T EAT

SNACKS: DELICIOUS / DECENT / DISGUSTING / DIDN'T EAT

QUIET   ANNOYED   COOL   SAD   TIRED   EXCITED   HAPPY   EMBARRASSED   SCARED

BORED   SICK   FRUSTRATED   ANGRY   FUNNY   PROUD   NERVOUS   GOOFY   SURPRISED

B = BEST PART OF YOUR DAY   **W** = WORST PART OF YOUR DAY   **M** = MOST OF THE DAY

RECORD IT
WHAT DID YOU LEARN TODAY?

MINIMUM FUNCTIONALITY

1) ABILITY	2) SKILL	3) VOCATION	4) RELATIONSHIP	5) MENTALITY
6) MENTAL EXERCISE	7) MUSCLE MEMORY	8) PRACTICE	9) TRAINING	10) EXPERIENCE

IN THIS CLASS	I ENGAGED MOST BY ...	MINIMUM FUNCTIONALITY	THIS CLASS	MAXIMUM POSSIBILITY
	THINKING SEEING LISTENING DOING			
	THINKING SEEING LISTENING DOING			
	THINKING SEEING LISTENING DOING			
	THINKING SEEING LISTENING DOING			
	THINKING SEEING LISTENING DOING			
	THINKING SEEING LISTENING DOING			
	THINKING SEEING LISTENING DOING			
	THINKING SEEING LISTENING DOING			

THIS INSTRUCTOR	BROUGHT ME THE MOST...
	EDUCATION
	TEACHING
	FUN
	CHALLENGES

THIS...	BROUGHT ME THE MOST ISSUES
CLASS	
CONCEPT	
LESSON	
INSTRUCTOR	

THIS CLASS	WAS THE MOST...
	EDUCATIONAL
	WORK
	FUN
	BORING

MAXIMUM POSSIBILITY

1) MOTIVATION	2) INSPIRATION	3) HIGHER EDUCATION	4) CAREER	5) DREAM
6) INVENTION	7) INNOVATION	8) NON-PROFIT	9) FORTUNE 500	10) SUPERHERO

RECORD IT
HOW WAS SCHOOL TODAY?

DATE:_____

HOW DID YOU GET ALONG WITH PEOPLE?

ALLIES: POSITIVE / NEGATIVE / NEUTRAL

ANNOYANCES: POSITIVE / NEGATIVE / NEUTRAL   INSTRUCTORS: POSITIVE / NEGATIVE / NEUTRAL

HOW DID YOU BEHAVE?

SUCCESSES: MAJOR / MINOR / NONE

STRUGGLES: MAJOR / MINOR / NONE

CONFESSIONS: MAJOR / MINOR / NONE

HOW WAS YOUR ENERGY?

MORNING: FULL TANK / HALF TANK / EMPTY   NOON: FULL TANK / HALF TANK / EMPTY

AFTERNOON: FULL TANK / HALF TANK / EMPTY

DID YOU NEED THE NURSE?

HEALTH: YES / NO   INJURY: YES / NO   PAIN: YES / NO

HOW WAS THE FOOD?

BREAKFAST: DELICIOUS / DECENT / DISGUSTING / DIDN'T EAT

LUNCH: DELICIOUS / DECENT / DISGUSTING / DIDN'T EAT

SNACKS: DELICIOUS / DECENT / DISGUSTING / DIDN'T EAT

QUIET   ANNOYED   COOL   SAD   TIRED   EXCITED   HAPPY   EMBARRASSED   SCARED

BORED   SICK   FRUSTRATED   ANGRY   FUNNY   PROUD   NERVOUS   GOOFY   SURPRISED

 **B** = BEST PART OF YOUR DAY   **W** = WORST PART OF YOUR DAY   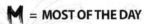 **M** = MOST OF THE DAY

RECORD IT
WHAT DID YOU LEARN TODAY?

1) ABILITY	2) SKILL	3) VOCATION	4) RELATIONSHIP	5) MENTALITY
6) MENTAL EXERCISE	7) MUSCLE MEMORY	8) PRACTICE	9) TRAINING	10) EXPERIENCE

IN THIS CLASS	I ENGAGED MOST BY ...	MINIMUM FUNCTIONALITY	THIS CLASS	MAXIMUM POSSIBILITY
	THINKING SEEING LISTENING DOING			
	THINKING SEEING LISTENING DOING			
	THINKING SEEING LISTENING DOING			
	THINKING SEEING LISTENING DOING			
	THINKING SEEING LISTENING DOING			
	THINKING SEEING LISTENING DOING			
	THINKING SEEING LISTENING DOING			
	THINKING SEEING LISTENING DOING			

THIS INSTRUCTOR	BROUGHT ME THE MOST...
	EDUCATION
	TEACHING
	FUN
	CHALLENGES

THIS...	BROUGHT ME THE MOST ISSUES
CLASS	
CONCEPT	
LESSON	
INSTRUCTOR	

THIS CLASS	WAS THE MOST...
	EDUCATIONAL
	WORK
	FUN
	BORING

MAXIMUM POSSIBILITY

1) MOTIVATION	2) INSPIRATION	3) HIGHER EDUCATION	4) CAREER	5) DREAM
6) INVENTION	7) INNOVATION	8) NON-PROFIT	9) FORTUNE 500	10) SUPERHERO

How Was School Today?

DATE:_____

HOW DID YOU GET ALONG WITH PEOPLE?

ALLIES: POSITIVE / NEGATIVE / NEUTRAL

ANNOYANCES: POSITIVE / NEGATIVE / NEUTRAL　　INSTRUCTORS: POSITIVE / NEGATIVE / NEUTRAL

HOW DID YOU BEHAVE?

SUCCESSES:　MAJOR / MINOR / NONE

STRUGGLES:　MAJOR / MINOR / NONE

CONFESSIONS: MAJOR / MINOR / NONE

HOW WAS YOUR ENERGY?

MORNING: FULL TANK / HALF TANK / EMPTY　　NOON: FULL TANK / HALF TANK / EMPTY

AFTERNOON: FULL TANK / HALF TANK / EMPTY

DID YOU NEED THE NURSE?

HEALTH: YES / NO　　INJURY: YES / NO　　PAIN: YES / NO

HOW WAS THE FOOD?

BREAKFAST: DELICIOUS / DECENT / DISGUSTING / DIDN'T EAT

LUNCH:　DELICIOUS / DECENT / DISGUSTING / DIDN'T EAT

SNACKS: DELICIOUS / DECENT / DISGUSTING / DIDN'T EAT

QUIET　　ANNOYED　　COOL　　SAD　　TIRED　　EXCITED　　HAPPY　　EMBARRASSED　　SCARED

BORED　　SICK　　FRUSTRATED　　ANGRY　　FUNNY　　PROUD　　NERVOUS　　GOOFY　　SURPRISED

B = BEST PART OF YOUR DAY　　W = WORST PART OF YOUR DAY　　M = MOST OF THE DAY

RECORD IT
WHAT DID YOU LEARN TODAY?

MINIMUM FUNCTIONALITY

1) ABILITY	2) SKILL	3) VOCATION	4) RELATIONSHIP	5) MENTALITY
6) MENTAL EXERCISE	7) MUSCLE MEMORY	8) PRACTICE	9) TRAINING	10) EXPERIENCE

IN THIS CLASS	I ENGAGED MOST BY ...	MINIMUM FUNCTIONALITY	THIS CLASS	MAXIMUM POSSIBILITY
	THINKING SEEING LISTENING DOING			
	THINKING SEEING LISTENING DOING			
	THINKING SEEING LISTENING DOING			
	THINKING SEEING LISTENING DOING			
	THINKING SEEING LISTENING DOING			
	THINKING SEEING LISTENING DOING			
	THINKING SEEING LISTENING DOING			
	THINKING SEEING LISTENING DOING			

THIS INSTRUCTOR	BROUGHT ME THE MOST...
	EDUCATION
	TEACHING
	FUN
	CHALLENGES

THIS...	BROUGHT ME THE MOST ISSUES
CLASS	
CONCEPT	
LESSON	
INSTRUCTOR	

THIS CLASS	WAS THE MOST...
	EDUCATIONAL
	WORK
	FUN
	BORING

MAXIMUM POSSIBILITY

1) MOTIVATION	2) INSPIRATION	3) HIGHER EDUCATION	4) CAREER	5) DREAM
6) INVENTION	7) INNOVATION	8) NON-PROFIT	9) FORTUNE 500	10) SUPERHERO

How Was School Today?

DATE:_____

HOW DID YOU GET ALONG WITH PEOPLE?

ALLIES: POSITIVE / NEGATIVE / NEUTRAL

ANNOYANCES: POSITIVE / NEGATIVE / NEUTRAL   INSTRUCTORS: POSITIVE / NEGATIVE / NEUTRAL

HOW DID YOU BEHAVE?

SUCCESSES: MAJOR / MINOR / NONE

STRUGGLES: MAJOR / MINOR / NONE

CONFESSIONS: MAJOR / MINOR / NONE

HOW WAS YOUR ENERGY?

MORNING: FULL TANK / HALF TANK / EMPTY   NOON: FULL TANK / HALF TANK / EMPTY

AFTERNOON: FULL TANK / HALF TANK / EMPTY

DID YOU NEED THE NURSE?

HEALTH: YES / NO   INJURY: YES / NO   PAIN: YES / NO

HOW WAS THE FOOD?

BREAKFAST: DELICIOUS / DECENT / DISGUSTING / DIDN'T EAT

LUNCH: DELICIOUS / DECENT / DISGUSTING / DIDN'T EAT

SNACKS: DELICIOUS / DECENT / DISGUSTING / DIDN'T EAT

QUIET   ANNOYED   COOL   SAD   TIRED   EXCITED   HAPPY   EMBARRASSED   SCARED

BORED   SICK   FRUSTRATED   ANGRY   FUNNY   PROUD   NERVOUS   GOOFY   SURPRISED

B = BEST PART OF YOUR DAY   **W** = WORST PART OF YOUR DAY   **M** = MOST OF THE DAY

RECORD IT
WHAT DID YOU LEARN TODAY?

MINIMUM FUNCTIONALITY

1) ABILITY	2) SKILL	3) VOCATION	4) RELATIONSHIP	5) MENTALITY
6) MENTAL EXERCISE	7) MUSCLE MEMORY	8) PRACTICE	9) TRAINING	10) EXPERIENCE

IN THIS CLASS	I ENGAGED MOST BY ...	MINIMUM FUNCTIONALITY	THIS CLASS	MAXIMUM POSSIBILITY
	THINKING SEEING LISTENING DOING			
	THINKING SEEING LISTENING DOING			
	THINKING SEEING LISTENING DOING			
	THINKING SEEING LISTENING DOING			
	THINKING SEEING LISTENING DOING			
	THINKING SEEING LISTENING DOING			
	THINKING SEEING LISTENING DOING			
	THINKING SEEING LISTENING DOING			

THIS INSTRUCTOR	BROUGHT ME THE MOST...
	EDUCATION
	TEACHING
	FUN
	CHALLENGES

THIS...	BROUGHT ME THE MOST ISSUES
CLASS	
CONCEPT	
LESSON	
INSTRUCTOR	

THIS CLASS	WAS THE MOST...
	EDUCATIONAL
	WORK
	FUN
	BORING

MAXIMUM POSSIBILITY

1) MOTIVATION	2) INSPIRATION	3) HIGHER EDUCATION	4) CAREER	5) DREAM
6) INVENTION	7) INNOVATION	8) NON-PROFIT	9) FORTUNE 500	10) SUPERHERO

RECORD IT
HOW WAS SCHOOL TODAY?

DATE:_____

HOW DID YOU GET ALONG WITH PEOPLE?

ALLIES: POSITIVE / NEGATIVE / NEUTRAL

ANNOYANCES: POSITIVE / NEGATIVE / NEUTRAL   INSTRUCTORS: POSITIVE / NEGATIVE / NEUTRAL

HOW DID YOU BEHAVE?

SUCCESSES: MAJOR / MINOR / NONE

STRUGGLES: MAJOR / MINOR / NONE

CONFESSIONS: MAJOR / MINOR / NONE

HOW WAS YOUR ENERGY?

MORNING: FULL TANK / HALF TANK / EMPTY   NOON: FULL TANK / HALF TANK / EMPTY

AFTERNOON: FULL TANK / HALF TANK / EMPTY

DID YOU NEED THE NURSE?

HEALTH: YES / NO   INJURY: YES / NO   PAIN: YES / NO

HOW WAS THE FOOD?

BREAKFAST: DELICIOUS / DECENT / DISGUSTING / DIDN'T EAT

LUNCH: DELICIOUS / DECENT / DISGUSTING / DIDN'T EAT

SNACKS: DELICIOUS / DECENT / DISGUSTING / DIDN'T EAT

 QUIET   ANNOYED   COOL   SAD   TIRED   EXCITED HAPPY EMBARRASSED SCARED

 BORED   SICK   FRUSTRATED   ANGRY   FUNNY   PROUD   NERVOUS   GOOFY   SURPRISED

B = BEST PART OF YOUR DAY   **W** = WORST PART OF YOUR DAY   **M** = MOST OF THE DAY

RECORD IT
WHAT DID YOU LEARN TODAY?

MINIMUM FUNCTIONALITY

1) ABILITY	2) SKILL	3) VOCATION	4) RELATIONSHIP	5) MENTALITY
6) MENTAL EXERCISE	7) MUSCLE MEMORY	8) PRACTICE	9) TRAINING	10) EXPERIENCE

IN THIS CLASS	I ENGAGED MOST BY ...		MINIMUM FUNCTIONALITY	THIS CLASS	MAXIMUM POSSIBILITY
	THINKING SEEING LISTENING DOING				
	THINKING SEEING LISTENING DOING				
	THINKING SEEING LISTENING DOING				
	THINKING SEEING LISTENING DOING				
	THINKING SEEING LISTENING DOING				
	THINKING SEEING LISTENING DOING				
	THINKING SEEING LISTENING DOING				
	THINKING SEEING LISTENING DOING				

THIS INSTRUCTOR	BROUGHT ME THE MOST...
	EDUCATION
	TEACHING
	FUN
	CHALLENGES

THIS...	BROUGHT ME THE MOST ISSUES
CLASS	
CONCEPT	
LESSON	
INSTRUCTOR	

THIS CLASS	WAS THE MOST...
	EDUCATIONAL
	WORK
	FUN
	BORING

MAXIMUM POSSIBILITY

1) MOTIVATION	2) INSPIRATION	3) HIGHER EDUCATION	4) CAREER	5) DREAM
6) INVENTION	7) INNOVATION	8) NON-PROFIT	9) FORTUNE 500	10) SUPERHERO

HOW WAS SCHOOL TODAY?

DATE:_____

HOW DID YOU GET ALONG WITH PEOPLE?

ALLIES: POSITIVE / NEGATIVE / NEUTRAL

ANNOYANCES: POSITIVE / NEGATIVE / NEUTRAL   INSTRUCTORS: POSITIVE / NEGATIVE / NEUTRAL

HOW DID YOU BEHAVE?

SUCCESSES: MAJOR / MINOR / NONE

STRUGGLES: MAJOR / MINOR / NONE

CONFESSIONS: MAJOR / MINOR / NONE

HOW WAS YOUR ENERGY?

MORNING: FULL TANK / HALF TANK / EMPTY   NOON: FULL TANK / HALF TANK / EMPTY

AFTERNOON: FULL TANK / HALF TANK / EMPTY

DID YOU NEED THE NURSE?

HEALTH: YES / NO   INJURY: YES / NO   PAIN: YES / NO

HOW WAS THE FOOD?

BREAKFAST: DELICIOUS / DECENT / DISGUSTING / DIDN'T EAT

LUNCH: DELICIOUS / DECENT / DISGUSTING / DIDN'T EAT

SNACKS: DELICIOUS / DECENT / DISGUSTING / DIDN'T EAT

 QUIET
 ANNOYED
 COOL
 SAD
 TIRED
 EXCITED
 HAPPY
 EMBARRASSED
 SCARED

 BORED
 SICK
 FRUSTRATED
 ANGRY
 FUNNY
 PROUD
 NERVOUS
 GOOFY
 SURPRISED

 B = BEST PART OF YOUR DAY   **W** = WORST PART OF YOUR DAY   **M** = MOST OF THE DAY

RECORD IT
WHAT DID YOU LEARN TODAY?

MINIMUM FUNCTIONALITY

1) ABILITY	2) SKILL	3) VOCATION	4) RELATIONSHIP	5) MENTALITY
6) MENTAL EXERCISE	7) MUSCLE MEMORY	8) PRACTICE	9) TRAINING	10) EXPERIENCE

IN THIS CLASS	I ENGAGED MOST BY ...	MINIMUM FUNCTIONALITY	THIS CLASS	MAXIMUM POSSIBILITY
	THINKING SEEING LISTENING DOING			
	THINKING SEEING LISTENING DOING			
	THINKING SEEING LISTENING DOING			
	THINKING SEEING LISTENING DOING			
	THINKING SEEING LISTENING DOING			
	THINKING SEEING LISTENING DOING			
	THINKING SEEING LISTENING DOING			
	THINKING SEEING LISTENING DOING			

THIS INSTRUCTOR	BROUGHT ME THE MOST...
	EDUCATION
	TEACHING
	FUN
	CHALLENGES

THIS...	BROUGHT ME THE MOST ISSUES
CLASS	
CONCEPT	
LESSON	
INSTRUCTOR	

THIS CLASS	WAS THE MOST...
	EDUCATIONAL
	WORK
	FUN
	BORING

MAXIMUM POSSIBILITY

1) MOTIVATION	2) INSPIRATION	3) HIGHER EDUCATION	4) CAREER	5) DREAM
6) INVENTION	7) INNOVATION	8) NON-PROFIT	9) FORTUNE 500	10) SUPERHERO

HOW WAS SCHOOL TODAY?

DATE:_____

HOW DID YOU GET ALONG WITH PEOPLE?

ALLIES: POSITIVE / NEGATIVE / NEUTRAL

ANNOYANCES: POSITIVE / NEGATIVE / NEUTRAL   INSTRUCTORS: POSITIVE / NEGATIVE / NEUTRAL

HOW DID YOU BEHAVE?

SUCCESSES: MAJOR / MINOR / NONE

STRUGGLES: MAJOR / MINOR / NONE

CONFESSIONS: MAJOR / MINOR / NONE

HOW WAS YOUR ENERGY?

MORNING: FULL TANK / HALF TANK / EMPTY   NOON: FULL TANK / HALF TANK / EMPTY

AFTERNOON: FULL TANK / HALF TANK / EMPTY

DID YOU NEED THE NURSE?

HEALTH: YES / NO   INJURY: YES / NO   PAIN: YES / NO

HOW WAS THE FOOD?

BREAKFAST: DELICIOUS / DECENT / DISGUSTING / DIDN'T EAT

LUNCH: DELICIOUS / DECENT / DISGUSTING / DIDN'T EAT

SNACKS: DELICIOUS / DECENT / DISGUSTING / DIDN'T EAT

QUIET   ANNOYED   COOL   SAD   TIRED   EXCITED   HAPPY   EMBARRASSED   SCARED

BORED   SICK   FRUSTRATED   ANGRY   FUNNY   PROUD   NERVOUS   GOOFY   SURPRISED

B = BEST PART OF YOUR DAY   **W** = WORST PART OF YOUR DAY   **M** = MOST OF THE DAY

RECORD IT
WHAT DID YOU LEARN TODAY?

MINIMUM FUNCTIONALITY

1) ABILITY	2) SKILL	3) VOCATION	4) RELATIONSHIP	5) MENTALITY
6) MENTAL EXERCISE	7) MUSCLE MEMORY	8) PRACTICE	9) TRAINING	10) EXPERIENCE

IN THIS CLASS	I ENGAGED MOST BY ...	MINIMUM FUNCTIONALITY	THIS CLASS	MAXIMUM POSSIBILITY
	THINKING SEEING LISTENING DOING			
	THINKING SEEING LISTENING DOING			
	THINKING SEEING LISTENING DOING			
	THINKING SEEING LISTENING DOING			
	THINKING SEEING LISTENING DOING			
	THINKING SEEING LISTENING DOING			
	THINKING SEEING LISTENING DOING			
	THINKING SEEING LISTENING DOING			

THIS INSTRUCTOR	BROUGHT ME THE MOST...
	EDUCATION
	TEACHING
	FUN
	CHALLENGES

THIS...	BROUGHT ME THE MOST ISSUES
CLASS	
CONCEPT	
LESSON	
INSTRUCTOR	

THIS CLASS	WAS THE MOST...
	EDUCATIONAL
	WORK
	FUN
	BORING

MAXIMUM POSSIBILITY

1) MOTIVATION	2) INSPIRATION	3) HIGHER EDUCATION	4) CAREER	5) DREAM
6) INVENTION	7) INNOVATION	8) NON-PROFIT	9) FORTUNE 500	10) SUPERHERO

RECORD IT
HOW WAS SCHOOL TODAY?

DATE:_____

HOW DID YOU GET ALONG WITH PEOPLE?

ALLIES: POSITIVE / NEGATIVE / NEUTRAL

ANNOYANCES: POSITIVE / NEGATIVE / NEUTRAL   INSTRUCTORS: POSITIVE / NEGATIVE / NEUTRAL

HOW DID YOU BEHAVE?

SUCCESSES: MAJOR / MINOR / NONE

STRUGGLES: MAJOR / MINOR / NONE

CONFESSIONS: MAJOR / MINOR / NONE

HOW WAS YOUR ENERGY?

MORNING: FULL TANK / HALF TANK / EMPTY   NOON: FULL TANK / HALF TANK / EMPTY

AFTERNOON: FULL TANK / HALF TANK / EMPTY

DID YOU NEED THE NURSE?

HEALTH: YES / NO   INJURY: YES / NO   PAIN: YES / NO

HOW WAS THE FOOD?

BREAKFAST: DELICIOUS / DECENT / DISGUSTING / DIDN'T EAT

LUNCH: DELICIOUS / DECENT / DISGUSTING / DIDN'T EAT

SNACKS: DELICIOUS / DECENT / DISGUSTING / DIDN'T EAT

 QUIET
 ANNOYED
 COOL
 SAD
 TIRED
 EXCITED
 HAPPY
 EMBARRASSED
 SCARED

 BORED
 SICK
 FRUSTRATED
 ANGRY
 FUNNY
 PROUD
 NERVOUS
 GOOFY
 SURPRISED

B = BEST PART OF YOUR DAY   **W** = WORST PART OF YOUR DAY   **M** = MOST OF THE DAY

RECORD IT
WHAT DID YOU LEARN TODAY?

1) ABILITY	2) SKILL	3) VOCATION	4) RELATIONSHIP	5) MENTALITY
6) MENTAL EXERCISE	7) MUSCLE MEMORY	8) PRACTICE	9) TRAINING	10) EXPERIENCE

IN THIS CLASS	I ENGAGED MOST BY ...	MINIMUM FUNCTIONALITY	THIS CLASS	MAXIMUM POSSIBILITY
	THINKING SEEING LISTENING DOING			
	THINKING SEEING LISTENING DOING			
	THINKING SEEING LISTENING DOING			
	THINKING SEEING LISTENING DOING			
	THINKING SEEING LISTENING DOING			
	THINKING SEEING LISTENING DOING			
	THINKING SEEING LISTENING DOING			
	THINKING SEEING LISTENING DOING			

THIS INSTRUCTOR	BROUGHT ME THE MOST...
	EDUCATION
	TEACHING
	FUN
	CHALLENGES

THIS...	BROUGHT ME THE MOST ISSUES
CLASS	
CONCEPT	
LESSON	
INSTRUCTOR	

THIS CLASS	WAS THE MOST...
	EDUCATIONAL
	WORK
	FUN
	BORING

MAXIMUM POSSIBILITY

1) MOTIVATION	2) INSPIRATION	3) HIGHER EDUCATION	4) CAREER	5) DREAM
6) INVENTION	7) INNOVATION	8) NON-PROFIT	9) FORTUNE 500	10) SUPERHERO

RECORD IT
How Was School Today?

DATE:_____

HOW DID YOU GET ALONG WITH PEOPLE?

ALLIES: POSITIVE / NEGATIVE / NEUTRAL

ANNOYANCES: POSITIVE / NEGATIVE / NEUTRAL   INSTRUCTORS: POSITIVE / NEGATIVE / NEUTRAL

HOW DID YOU BEHAVE?

SUCCESSES: MAJOR / MINOR / NONE

STRUGGLES: MAJOR / MINOR / NONE

CONFESSIONS: MAJOR / MINOR / NONE

HOW WAS YOUR ENERGY?

MORNING: FULL TANK / HALF TANK / EMPTY   NOON: FULL TANK / HALF TANK / EMPTY

AFTERNOON: FULL TANK / HALF TANK / EMPTY

DID YOU NEED THE NURSE?

HEALTH: YES / NO   INJURY: YES / NO   PAIN: YES / NO

HOW WAS THE FOOD?

BREAKFAST: DELICIOUS / DECENT / DISGUSTING / DIDN'T EAT

LUNCH: DELICIOUS / DECENT / DISGUSTING / DIDN'T EAT

SNACKS: DELICIOUS / DECENT / DISGUSTING / DIDN'T EAT

QUIET   ANNOYED   COOL   SAD   TIRED   EXCITED   HAPPY   EMBARRASSED   SCARED

BORED   SICK   FRUSTRATED   ANGRY   FUNNY   PROUD   NERVOUS   GOOFY   SURPRISED

B = BEST PART OF YOUR DAY   W = WORST PART OF YOUR DAY   M = MOST OF THE DAY

RECORD IT
WHAT DID YOU LEARN TODAY?

MINIMUM FUNCTIONALITY

1) ABILITY	2) SKILL	3) VOCATION	4) RELATIONSHIP	5) MENTALITY
6) MENTAL EXERCISE	7) MUSCLE MEMORY	8) PRACTICE	9) TRAINING	10) EXPERIENCE

IN THIS CLASS	I ENGAGED MOST BY ...	MINIMUM FUNCTIONALITY	THIS CLASS	MAXIMUM POSSIBILITY
	THINKING SEEING LISTENING DOING			
	THINKING SEEING LISTENING DOING			
	THINKING SEEING LISTENING DOING			
	THINKING SEEING LISTENING DOING			
	THINKING SEEING LISTENING DOING			
	THINKING SEEING LISTENING DOING			
	THINKING SEEING LISTENING DOING			
	THINKING SEEING LISTENING DOING			

THIS INSTRUCTOR	BROUGHT ME THE MOST...
	EDUCATION
	TEACHING
	FUN
	CHALLENGES

THIS...	BROUGHT ME THE MOST ISSUES
CLASS	
CONCEPT	
LESSON	
INSTRUCTOR	

THIS CLASS	WAS THE MOST...
	EDUCATIONAL
	WORK
	FUN
	BORING

MAXIMUM POSSIBILITY

1) MOTIVATION	2) INSPIRATION	3) HIGHER EDUCATION	4) CAREER	5) DREAM
6) INVENTION	7) INNOVATION	8) NON-PROFIT	9) FORTUNE 500	10) SUPERHERO

PROGRESS REPORT

1) When I think about my interactions with people this quarter, I see that:
    I was successful…_____

    _____

    I really struggled…_____

    _____

    Moving forward…_____

    _____

    I may need my allies…_____

    _____

2) When I think about my behavior this quarter, I see that:
    I was successful…_____

    _____

    I really struggled…_____

    _____

    Moving forward…_____

    _____

    I may need my allies…_____

    _____

3) When I think about my overall health this quarter, I see that:
    I was successful…_____

    _____

    I really struggled…_____

    _____

    Moving forward…_____

    _____

    I may need my allies…_____

    _____

4) When I think about my eating habits this quarter, I see that:
    I was successful…_____

    _____

    I really struggled…_____

    _____

    Moving forward…_____

    _____

    I may need my allies…_____

    _____

5) When I think about my overall experience in school this quarter, I see that:
    I was successful…_____

    _____

    I really struggled…_____

    _____

    Moving forward…_____

    _____

    I may need my allies…_____

    _____

PROGRESS REPORT

6) When I think about how I engaged in classes this quarter, I see that:
I was successful…_____
_____
I really struggled…_____
_____
Moving forward…_____
_____
I may need my allies…_____
_____

7) When I think about the educational value of class experiences this quarter, I see that:
I was successful…_____
_____
I really struggled…_____
_____
Moving forward…_____
_____
I may need my allies…_____
_____

8) When I think about how my instructors did this quarter, I see that:
I was successful…_____
_____
I really struggled…_____
_____
Moving forward…_____
_____
I may need my allies…_____
_____

9) When I think about academic issues I had this quarter, I see that:
I was successful…_____
_____
I really struggled…_____
_____
Moving forward…_____
_____
I may need my allies…_____
_____

10) When I think about how my classes went this quarter, I see that:
I was successful…_____
_____
I really struggled…_____
_____
Moving forward…_____
_____
I may need my allies…_____
_____

STUDENT NAME / GRADE / SCHOOL NAME

SCHOOL YEAR

20 ___ / ___ 20 ___

QUARTER

FIRST   SECOND   THIRD   FOURTH

CLASS SCHEDULE

CLASS	TEACHER	ROOM #	TIME

RECORD IT
How Was School Today?

DATE:_____

HOW DID YOU GET ALONG WITH PEOPLE?

ALLIES: POSITIVE / NEGATIVE / NEUTRAL

ANNOYANCES: POSITIVE / NEGATIVE / NEUTRAL   INSTRUCTORS: POSITIVE / NEGATIVE / NEUTRAL

HOW DID YOU BEHAVE?

SUCCESSES: MAJOR / MINOR / NONE

STRUGGLES: MAJOR / MINOR / NONE

CONFESSIONS: MAJOR / MINOR / NONE

HOW WAS YOUR ENERGY?

MORNING: FULL TANK / HALF TANK / EMPTY   NOON: FULL TANK / HALF TANK / EMPTY

AFTERNOON: FULL TANK / HALF TANK / EMPTY

DID YOU NEED THE NURSE?

HEALTH: YES / NO   INJURY: YES / NO   PAIN: YES / NO

HOW WAS THE FOOD?

BREAKFAST: DELICIOUS / DECENT / DISGUSTING / DIDN'T EAT

LUNCH: DELICIOUS / DECENT / DISGUSTING / DIDN'T EAT

SNACKS: DELICIOUS / DECENT / DISGUSTING / DIDN'T EAT

 QUIET
 ANNOYED
 COOL
 SAD
 TIRED
 EXCITED
 HAPPY
 EMBARRASSED
 SCARED

 BORED
 SICK
 FRUSTRATED
 ANGRY
 FUNNY
 PROUD
 NERVOUS
 GOOFY
 SURPRISED

B = BEST PART OF YOUR DAY   **W** = WORST PART OF YOUR DAY   **M** = MOST OF THE DAY

RECORD IT
WHAT DID YOU LEARN TODAY?

MINIMUM FUNCTIONALITY

1) ABILITY	2) SKILL	3) VOCATION	4) RELATIONSHIP	5) MENTALITY
6) MENTAL EXERCISE	7) MUSCLE MEMORY	8) PRACTICE	9) TRAINING	10) EXPERIENCE

IN THIS CLASS	I ENGAGED MOST BY ...	MINIMUM FUNCTIONALITY	THIS CLASS	MAXIMUM POSSIBILITY
	THINKING SEEING LISTENING DOING			
	THINKING SEEING LISTENING DOING			
	THINKING SEEING LISTENING DOING			
	THINKING SEEING LISTENING DOING			
	THINKING SEEING LISTENING DOING			
	THINKING SEEING LISTENING DOING			
	THINKING SEEING LISTENING DOING			
	THINKING SEEING LISTENING DOING			

THIS INSTRUCTOR	BROUGHT ME THE MOST...
	EDUCATION
	TEACHING
	FUN
	CHALLENGES

THIS...	BROUGHT ME THE MOST ISSUES
CLASS	
CONCEPT	
LESSON	
INSTRUCTOR	

THIS CLASS	WAS THE MOST...
	EDUCATIONAL
	WORK
	FUN
	BORING

MAXIMUM POSSIBILITY

1) MOTIVATION	2) INSPIRATION	3) HIGHER EDUCATION	4) CAREER	5) DREAM
6) INVENTION	7) INNOVATION	8) NON-PROFIT	9) FORTUNE 500	10) SUPERHERO

RECORD IT
HOW WAS SCHOOL TODAY?

DATE:_____

HOW DID YOU GET ALONG WITH PEOPLE?

ALLIES: POSITIVE / NEGATIVE / NEUTRAL

ANNOYANCES: POSITIVE / NEGATIVE / NEUTRAL   INSTRUCTORS: POSITIVE / NEGATIVE / NEUTRAL

HOW DID YOU BEHAVE?

SUCCESSES: MAJOR / MINOR / NONE

STRUGGLES: MAJOR / MINOR / NONE

CONFESSIONS: MAJOR / MINOR / NONE

HOW WAS YOUR ENERGY?

MORNING: FULL TANK / HALF TANK / EMPTY   NOON: FULL TANK / HALF TANK / EMPTY

AFTERNOON: FULL TANK / HALF TANK / EMPTY

DID YOU NEED THE NURSE?

HEALTH: YES / NO   INJURY: YES / NO   PAIN: YES / NO

HOW WAS THE FOOD?

BREAKFAST: DELICIOUS / DECENT / DISGUSTING / DIDN'T EAT

LUNCH: DELICIOUS / DECENT / DISGUSTING / DIDN'T EAT

SNACKS: DELICIOUS / DECENT / DISGUSTING / DIDN'T EAT

QUIET   ANNOYED   COOL   SAD   TIRED   EXCITED   HAPPY   EMBARRASSED   SCARED

BORED   SICK   FRUSTRATED   ANGRY   FUNNY   PROUD   NERVOUS   GOOFY   SURPRISED

B = BEST PART OF YOUR DAY   **W** = WORST PART OF YOUR DAY   **M** = MOST OF THE DAY

RECORD IT
WHAT DID YOU LEARN TODAY?

MINIMUM FUNCTIONALITY

1) ABILITY	2) SKILL	3) VOCATION	4) RELATIONSHIP	5) MENTALITY
6) MENTAL EXERCISE	7) MUSCLE MEMORY	8) PRACTICE	9) TRAINING	10) EXPERIENCE

IN THIS CLASS	I ENGAGED MOST BY …	MINIMUM FUNCTIONALITY	THIS CLASS	MAXIMUM POSSIBILITY
	THINKING SEEING LISTENING DOING			
	THINKING SEEING LISTENING DOING			
	THINKING SEEING LISTENING DOING			
	THINKING SEEING LISTENING DOING			
	THINKING SEEING LISTENING DOING			
	THINKING SEEING LISTENING DOING			
	THINKING SEEING LISTENING DOING			
	THINKING SEEING LISTENING DOING			

THIS INSTRUCTOR	BROUGHT ME THE MOST…
	EDUCATION
	TEACHING
	FUN
	CHALLENGES

THIS…	BROUGHT ME THE MOST ISSUES
CLASS	
CONCEPT	
LESSON	
INSTRUCTOR	

THIS CLASS	WAS THE MOST…
	EDUCATIONAL
	WORK
	FUN
	BORING

MAXIMUM POSSIBILITY

1) MOTIVATION	2) INSPIRATION	3) HIGHER EDUCATION	4) CAREER	5) DREAM
6) INVENTION	7) INNOVATION	8) NON-PROFIT	9) FORTUNE 500	10) SUPERHERO

RECORD IT
How Was School Today?

DATE:_____

HOW DID YOU GET ALONG WITH PEOPLE?

ALLIES: POSITIVE / NEGATIVE / NEUTRAL

ANNOYANCES: POSITIVE / NEGATIVE / NEUTRAL   INSTRUCTORS: POSITIVE / NEGATIVE / NEUTRAL

HOW DID YOU BEHAVE?

SUCCESSES: MAJOR / MINOR / NONE

STRUGGLES: MAJOR / MINOR / NONE

CONFESSIONS: MAJOR / MINOR / NONE

HOW WAS YOUR ENERGY?

MORNING: FULL TANK / HALF TANK / EMPTY   NOON: FULL TANK / HALF TANK / EMPTY

AFTERNOON: FULL TANK / HALF TANK / EMPTY

DID YOU NEED THE NURSE?

HEALTH: YES / NO   INJURY: YES / NO   PAIN: YES / NO

HOW WAS THE FOOD?

BREAKFAST: DELICIOUS / DECENT / DISGUSTING / DIDN'T EAT

LUNCH: DELICIOUS / DECENT / DISGUSTING / DIDN'T EAT

SNACKS: DELICIOUS / DECENT / DISGUSTING / DIDN'T EAT

 QUIET
 ANNOYED
 COOL
 SAD
 TIRED
 EXCITED
 HAPPY
 EMBARRASSED
 SCARED

 BORED
 SICK
 FRUSTRATED
 ANGRY
 FUNNY
 PROUD
 NERVOUS
 GOOFY
 SURPRISED

B = BEST PART OF YOUR DAY   W = WORST PART OF YOUR DAY   M = MOST OF THE DAY

RECORD IT
WHAT DID YOU LEARN TODAY?

MINIMUM FUNCTIONALITY

1) ABILITY	2) SKILL	3) VOCATION	4) RELATIONSHIP	5) MENTALITY
6) MENTAL EXERCISE	7) MUSCLE MEMORY	8) PRACTICE	9) TRAINING	10) EXPERIENCE

IN THIS CLASS	I ENGAGED MOST BY ...	MINIMUM FUNCTIONALITY	THIS CLASS	MAXIMUM POSSIBILITY
	THINKING SEEING LISTENING DOING			
	THINKING SEEING LISTENING DOING			
	THINKING SEEING LISTENING DOING			
	THINKING SEEING LISTENING DOING			
	THINKING SEEING LISTENING DOING			
	THINKING SEEING LISTENING DOING			
	THINKING SEEING LISTENING DOING			
	THINKING SEEING LISTENING DOING			

THIS INSTRUCTOR	BROUGHT ME THE MOST...
	EDUCATION
	TEACHING
	FUN
	CHALLENGES

THIS...	BROUGHT ME THE MOST ISSUES
CLASS	
CONCEPT	
LESSON	
INSTRUCTOR	

THIS CLASS	WAS THE MOST...
	EDUCATIONAL
	WORK
	FUN
	BORING

MAXIMUM POSSIBILITY

1) MOTIVATION	2) INSPIRATION	3) HIGHER EDUCATION	4) CAREER	5) DREAM
6) INVENTION	7) INNOVATION	8) NON-PROFIT	9) FORTUNE 500	10) SUPERHERO

RECORD IT
HOW WAS SCHOOL TODAY?

DATE:_____

HOW DID YOU GET ALONG WITH PEOPLE?

ALLIES: POSITIVE / NEGATIVE / NEUTRAL

ANNOYANCES: POSITIVE / NEGATIVE / NEUTRAL   INSTRUCTORS: POSITIVE / NEGATIVE / NEUTRAL

HOW DID YOU BEHAVE?

SUCCESSES: MAJOR / MINOR / NONE

STRUGGLES: MAJOR / MINOR / NONE

CONFESSIONS: MAJOR / MINOR / NONE

HOW WAS YOUR ENERGY?

MORNING: FULL TANK / HALF TANK / EMPTY   NOON: FULL TANK / HALF TANK / EMPTY

AFTERNOON: FULL TANK / HALF TANK / EMPTY

DID YOU NEED THE NURSE?

HEALTH: YES / NO   INJURY: YES / NO   PAIN: YES / NO

HOW WAS THE FOOD?

BREAKFAST: DELICIOUS / DECENT / DISGUSTING / DIDN'T EAT

LUNCH: DELICIOUS / DECENT / DISGUSTING / DIDN'T EAT

SNACKS: DELICIOUS / DECENT / DISGUSTING / DIDN'T EAT

QUIET   ANNOYED   COOL   SAD   TIRED   EXCITED   HAPPY   EMBARRASSED   SCARED

BORED   SICK   FRUSTRATED   ANGRY   FUNNY   PROUD   NERVOUS   GOOFY   SURPRISED

B = BEST PART OF YOUR DAY   **W** = WORST PART OF YOUR DAY   **M** = MOST OF THE DAY

RECORD IT
WHAT DID YOU LEARN TODAY?

MINIMUM FUNCTIONALITY

1) ABILITY	2) SKILL	3) VOCATION	4) RELATIONSHIP	5) MENTALITY
6) MENTAL EXERCISE	7) MUSCLE MEMORY	8) PRACTICE	9) TRAINING	10) EXPERIENCE

IN THIS CLASS	I ENGAGED MOST BY ...	MINIMUM FUNCTIONALITY	THIS CLASS	MAXIMUM POSSIBILITY
	THINKING SEEING LISTENING DOING			
	THINKING SEEING LISTENING DOING			
	THINKING SEEING LISTENING DOING			
	THINKING SEEING LISTENING DOING			
	THINKING SEEING LISTENING DOING			
	THINKING SEEING LISTENING DOING			
	THINKING SEEING LISTENING DOING			
	THINKING SEEING LISTENING DOING			

THIS INSTRUCTOR	BROUGHT ME THE MOST...
	EDUCATION
	TEACHING
	FUN
	CHALLENGES

THIS...	BROUGHT ME THE MOST ISSUES
CLASS	
CONCEPT	
LESSON	
INSTRUCTOR	

THIS CLASS	WAS THE MOST...
	EDUCATIONAL
	WORK
	FUN
	BORING

MAXIMUM POSSIBILITY

1) MOTIVATION	2) INSPIRATION	3) HIGHER EDUCATION	4) CAREER	5) DREAM
6) INVENTION	7) INNOVATION	8) NON-PROFIT	9) FORTUNE 500	10) SUPERHERO

RECORD IT

HOW WAS SCHOOL TODAY?

DATE:_____

HOW DID YOU GET ALONG WITH PEOPLE?

ALLIES: POSITIVE / NEGATIVE / NEUTRAL

ANNOYANCES: POSITIVE / NEGATIVE / NEUTRAL   INSTRUCTORS: POSITIVE / NEGATIVE / NEUTRAL

HOW DID YOU BEHAVE?

SUCCESSES: MAJOR / MINOR / NONE

STRUGGLES: MAJOR / MINOR / NONE

CONFESSIONS: MAJOR / MINOR / NONE

HOW WAS YOUR ENERGY?

MORNING: FULL TANK / HALF TANK / EMPTY   NOON: FULL TANK / HALF TANK / EMPTY

AFTERNOON: FULL TANK / HALF TANK / EMPTY

DID YOU NEED THE NURSE?

HEALTH: YES / NO   INJURY: YES / NO   PAIN: YES / NO

HOW WAS THE FOOD?

BREAKFAST: DELICIOUS / DECENT / DISGUSTING / DIDN'T EAT

LUNCH: DELICIOUS / DECENT / DISGUSTING / DIDN'T EAT

SNACKS: DELICIOUS / DECENT / DISGUSTING / DIDN'T EAT

QUIET   ANNOYED   COOL   SAD   TIRED   EXCITED   HAPPY   EMBARRASSED   SCARED

BORED   SICK   FRUSTRATED   ANGRY   FUNNY   PROUD   NERVOUS   GOOFY   SURPRISED

B = BEST PART OF YOUR DAY   **W** = WORST PART OF YOUR DAY   **M** = MOST OF THE DAY

RECORD IT
WHAT DID YOU LEARN TODAY?

MINIMUM FUNCTIONALITY

1) ABILITY	2) SKILL	3) VOCATION	4) RELATIONSHIP	5) MENTALITY
6) MENTAL EXERCISE	7) MUSCLE MEMORY	8) PRACTICE	9) TRAINING	10) EXPERIENCE

IN THIS CLASS	I ENGAGED MOST BY …	MINIMUM FUNCTIONALITY	THIS CLASS	MAXIMUM POSSIBILITY
	THINKING SEEING LISTENING DOING			
	THINKING SEEING LISTENING DOING			
	THINKING SEEING LISTENING DOING			
	THINKING SEEING LISTENING DOING			
	THINKING SEEING LISTENING DOING			
	THINKING SEEING LISTENING DOING			
	THINKING SEEING LISTENING DOING			
	THINKING SEEING LISTENING DOING			

THIS INSTRUCTOR	BROUGHT ME THE MOST...
	EDUCATION
	TEACHING
	FUN
	CHALLENGES

THIS...	BROUGHT ME THE MOST ISSUES
CLASS	
CONCEPT	
LESSON	
INSTRUCTOR	

THIS CLASS	WAS THE MOST...
	EDUCATIONAL
	WORK
	FUN
	BORING

MAXIMUM POSSIBILITY

1) MOTIVATION	2) INSPIRATION	3) HIGHER EDUCATION	4) CAREER	5) DREAM
6) INVENTION	7) INNOVATION	8) NON-PROFIT	9) FORTUNE 500	10) SUPERHERO

RECORD IT
HOW WAS SCHOOL TODAY?

DATE:_____

HOW DID YOU GET ALONG WITH PEOPLE?

ALLIES: POSITIVE / NEGATIVE / NEUTRAL

ANNOYANCES: POSITIVE / NEGATIVE / NEUTRAL   INSTRUCTORS: POSITIVE / NEGATIVE / NEUTRAL

HOW DID YOU BEHAVE?

SUCCESSES: MAJOR / MINOR / NONE

STRUGGLES: MAJOR / MINOR / NONE

CONFESSIONS: MAJOR / MINOR / NONE

HOW WAS YOUR ENERGY?

MORNING: FULL TANK / HALF TANK / EMPTY   NOON: FULL TANK / HALF TANK / EMPTY

AFTERNOON: FULL TANK / HALF TANK / EMPTY

DID YOU NEED THE NURSE?

HEALTH: YES / NO   INJURY: YES / NO   PAIN: YES / NO

HOW WAS THE FOOD?

BREAKFAST: DELICIOUS / DECENT / DISGUSTING / DIDN'T EAT

LUNCH: DELICIOUS / DECENT / DISGUSTING / DIDN'T EAT

SNACKS: DELICIOUS / DECENT / DISGUSTING / DIDN'T EAT

QUIET   ANNOYED   COOL   SAD   TIRED   EXCITED   HAPPY   EMBARRASSED   SCARED

BORED   SICK   FRUSTRATED   ANGRY   FUNNY   PROUD   NERVOUS   GOOFY   SURPRISED

B = BEST PART OF YOUR DAY   **W** = WORST PART OF YOUR DAY   **M** = MOST OF THE DAY

RECORD IT
WHAT DID YOU LEARN TODAY?

MINIMUM FUNCTIONALITY

1) ABILITY	2) SKILL	3) VOCATION	4) RELATIONSHIP	5) MENTALITY
6) MENTAL EXERCISE	7) MUSCLE MEMORY	8) PRACTICE	9) TRAINING	10) EXPERIENCE

IN THIS CLASS	I ENGAGED MOST BY ...	MINIMUM FUNCTIONALITY	THIS CLASS	MAXIMUM POSSIBILITY
	THINKING SEEING LISTENING DOING			
	THINKING SEEING LISTENING DOING			
	THINKING SEEING LISTENING DOING			
	THINKING SEEING LISTENING DOING			
	THINKING SEEING LISTENING DOING			
	THINKING SEEING LISTENING DOING			
	THINKING SEEING LISTENING DOING			
	THINKING SEEING LISTENING DOING			

THIS INSTRUCTOR	BROUGHT ME THE MOST...
	EDUCATION
	TEACHING
	FUN
	CHALLENGES

THIS...	BROUGHT ME THE MOST ISSUES
CLASS	
CONCEPT	
LESSON	
INSTRUCTOR	

THIS CLASS	WAS THE MOST...
	EDUCATIONAL
	WORK
	FUN
	BORING

MAXIMUM POSSIBILITY

1) MOTIVATION	2) INSPIRATION	3) HIGHER EDUCATION	4) CAREER	5) DREAM
6) INVENTION	7) INNOVATION	8) NON-PROFIT	9) FORTUNE 500	10) SUPERHERO

RECORD IT
How Was School Today?

DATE:_____

HOW DID YOU GET ALONG WITH PEOPLE?

ALLIES: POSITIVE / NEGATIVE / NEUTRAL

ANNOYANCES: POSITIVE / NEGATIVE / NEUTRAL   INSTRUCTORS: POSITIVE / NEGATIVE / NEUTRAL

HOW DID YOU BEHAVE?

SUCCESSES: MAJOR / MINOR / NONE

STRUGGLES: MAJOR / MINOR / NONE

CONFESSIONS: MAJOR / MINOR / NONE

HOW WAS YOUR ENERGY?

MORNING: FULL TANK / HALF TANK / EMPTY   NOON: FULL TANK / HALF TANK / EMPTY

AFTERNOON: FULL TANK / HALF TANK / EMPTY

DID YOU NEED THE NURSE?

HEALTH: YES / NO   INJURY: YES / NO   PAIN: YES / NO

HOW WAS THE FOOD?

BREAKFAST: DELICIOUS / DECENT / DISGUSTING / DIDN'T EAT

LUNCH: DELICIOUS / DECENT / DISGUSTING / DIDN'T EAT

SNACKS: DELICIOUS / DECENT / DISGUSTING / DIDN'T EAT

QUIET   ANNOYED   COOL   SAD   TIRED   EXCITED   HAPPY   EMBARRASSED   SCARED

BORED   SICK   FRUSTRATED   ANGRY   FUNNY   PROUD   NERVOUS   GOOFY   SURPRISED

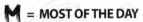

B = BEST PART OF YOUR DAY   W = WORST PART OF YOUR DAY   M = MOST OF THE DAY

RECORD IT
WHAT DID YOU LEARN TODAY?

MINIMUM FUNCTIONALITY

1) ABILITY	2) SKILL	3) VOCATION	4) RELATIONSHIP	5) MENTALITY
6) MENTAL EXERCISE	7) MUSCLE MEMORY	8) PRACTICE	9) TRAINING	10) EXPERIENCE

IN THIS CLASS	I ENGAGED MOST BY ...	MINIMUM FUNCTIONALITY	THIS CLASS	MAXIMUM POSSIBILITY
	THINKING SEEING LISTENING DOING			
	THINKING SEEING LISTENING DOING			
	THINKING SEEING LISTENING DOING			
	THINKING SEEING LISTENING DOING			
	THINKING SEEING LISTENING DOING			
	THINKING SEEING LISTENING DOING			
	THINKING SEEING LISTENING DOING			
	THINKING SEEING LISTENING DOING			

THIS INSTRUCTOR	BROUGHT ME THE MOST...
	EDUCATION
	TEACHING
	FUN
	CHALLENGES

THIS...	BROUGHT ME THE MOST ISSUES
CLASS	
CONCEPT	
LESSON	
INSTRUCTOR	

THIS CLASS	WAS THE MOST...
	EDUCATIONAL
	WORK
	FUN
	BORING

MAXIMUM POSSIBILITY

1) MOTIVATION	2) INSPIRATION	3) HIGHER EDUCATION	4) CAREER	5) DREAM
6) INVENTION	7) INNOVATION	8) NON-PROFIT	9) FORTUNE 500	10) SUPERHERO

RECORD IT
How Was School Today?

DATE:_____

HOW DID YOU GET ALONG WITH PEOPLE?

ALLIES: POSITIVE / NEGATIVE / NEUTRAL

ANNOYANCES: POSITIVE / NEGATIVE / NEUTRAL   INSTRUCTORS: POSITIVE / NEGATIVE / NEUTRAL

HOW DID YOU BEHAVE?

SUCCESSES: MAJOR / MINOR / NONE

STRUGGLES: MAJOR / MINOR / NONE

CONFESSIONS: MAJOR / MINOR / NONE

HOW WAS YOUR ENERGY?

MORNING: FULL TANK / HALF TANK / EMPTY   NOON: FULL TANK / HALF TANK / EMPTY

AFTERNOON: FULL TANK / HALF TANK / EMPTY

DID YOU NEED THE NURSE?

HEALTH: YES / NO   INJURY: YES / NO   PAIN: YES / NO

HOW WAS THE FOOD?

BREAKFAST: DELICIOUS / DECENT / DISGUSTING / DIDN'T EAT

LUNCH: DELICIOUS / DECENT / DISGUSTING / DIDN'T EAT

SNACKS: DELICIOUS / DECENT / DISGUSTING / DIDN'T EAT

QUIET   ANNOYED   COOL   SAD   TIRED   EXCITED   HAPPY   EMBARRASSED   SCARED

BORED   SICK   FRUSTRATED   ANGRY   FUNNY   PROUD   NERVOUS   GOOFY   SURPRISED

B = BEST PART OF YOUR DAY   **W** = WORST PART OF YOUR DAY   **M** = MOST OF THE DAY

RECORD IT
WHAT DID YOU LEARN TODAY?

MINIMUM FUNCTIONALITY

1) ABILITY	2) SKILL	3) VOCATION	4) RELATIONSHIP	5) MENTALITY
6) MENTAL EXERCISE	7) MUSCLE MEMORY	8) PRACTICE	9) TRAINING	10) EXPERIENCE

IN THIS CLASS	I ENGAGED MOST BY ...		MINIMUM FUNCTIONALITY	THIS CLASS	MAXIMUM POSSIBILITY
	THINKING SEEING LISTENING DOING				
	THINKING SEEING LISTENING DOING				
	THINKING SEEING LISTENING DOING				
	THINKING SEEING LISTENING DOING				
	THINKING SEEING LISTENING DOING				
	THINKING SEEING LISTENING DOING				
	THINKING SEEING LISTENING DOING				
	THINKING SEEING LISTENING DOING				

THIS INSTRUCTOR	BROUGHT ME THE MOST...
	EDUCATION
	TEACHING
	FUN
	CHALLENGES

THIS...	BROUGHT ME THE MOST ISSUES
CLASS	
CONCEPT	
LESSON	
INSTRUCTOR	

THIS CLASS	WAS THE MOST...
	EDUCATIONAL
	WORK
	FUN
	BORING

MAXIMUM POSSIBILITY

1) MOTIVATION	2) INSPIRATION	3) HIGHER EDUCATION	4) CAREER	5) DREAM
6) INVENTION	7) INNOVATION	8) NON-PROFIT	9) FORTUNE 500	10) SUPERHERO

RECORD IT
How Was School Today?

DATE:_____

HOW DID YOU GET ALONG WITH PEOPLE?

ALLIES: POSITIVE / NEGATIVE / NEUTRAL

ANNOYANCES: POSITIVE / NEGATIVE / NEUTRAL   INSTRUCTORS: POSITIVE / NEGATIVE / NEUTRAL

HOW DID YOU BEHAVE?

SUCCESSES: MAJOR / MINOR / NONE

STRUGGLES: MAJOR / MINOR / NONE

CONFESSIONS: MAJOR / MINOR / NONE

HOW WAS YOUR ENERGY?

MORNING: FULL TANK / HALF TANK / EMPTY   NOON: FULL TANK / HALF TANK / EMPTY

AFTERNOON: FULL TANK / HALF TANK / EMPTY

DID YOU NEED THE NURSE?

HEALTH: YES / NO   INJURY: YES / NO   PAIN: YES / NO

HOW WAS THE FOOD?

BREAKFAST: DELICIOUS / DECENT / DISGUSTING / DIDN'T EAT

LUNCH: DELICIOUS / DECENT / DISGUSTING / DIDN'T EAT

SNACKS: DELICIOUS / DECENT / DISGUSTING / DIDN'T EAT

 QUIET
 ANNOYED
 COOL
 SAD
 TIRED
 EXCITED
 HAPPY
 EMBARRASSED
 SCARED

 BORED
SICK
FRUSTRATED
ANGRY
 FUNNY
 PROUD
 NERVOUS
 GOOFY
 SURPRISED

 B = BEST PART OF YOUR DAY   W = WORST PART OF YOUR DAY   M = MOST OF THE DAY

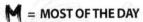

RECORD IT
WHAT DID YOU LEARN TODAY?

MINIMUM FUNCTIONALITY

| 1) ABILITY | 2) SKILL | 3) VOCATION | 4) RELATIONSHIP | 5) MENTALITY |
| 6) MENTAL EXERCISE | 7) MUSCLE MEMORY | 8) PRACTICE | 9) TRAINING | 10) EXPERIENCE |

IN THIS CLASS	I ENGAGED MOST BY …	MINIMUM FUNCTIONALITY	THIS CLASS	MAXIMUM POSSIBILITY
	THINKING SEEING LISTENING DOING			
	THINKING SEEING LISTENING DOING			
	THINKING SEEING LISTENING DOING			
	THINKING SEEING LISTENING DOING			
	THINKING SEEING LISTENING DOING			
	THINKING SEEING LISTENING DOING			
	THINKING SEEING LISTENING DOING			
	THINKING SEEING LISTENING DOING			

THIS INSTRUCTOR	BROUGHT ME THE MOST...
	EDUCATION
	TEACHING
	FUN
	CHALLENGES

THIS...	BROUGHT ME THE MOST ISSUES
CLASS	
CONCEPT	
LESSON	
INSTRUCTOR	

THIS CLASS	WAS THE MOST...
	EDUCATIONAL
	WORK
	FUN
	BORING

MAXIMUM POSSIBILITY

| 1) MOTIVATION | 2) INSPIRATION | 3) HIGHER EDUCATION | 4) CAREER | 5) DREAM |
| 6) INVENTION | 7) INNOVATION | 8) NON-PROFIT | 9) FORTUNE 500 | 10) SUPERHERO |

RECORD IT
HOW WAS SCHOOL TODAY?

DATE:_____

HOW DID YOU GET ALONG WITH PEOPLE?

ALLIES: POSITIVE / NEGATIVE / NEUTRAL

ANNOYANCES: POSITIVE / NEGATIVE / NEUTRAL   INSTRUCTORS: POSITIVE / NEGATIVE / NEUTRAL

HOW DID YOU BEHAVE?

SUCCESSES: MAJOR / MINOR / NONE

STRUGGLES: MAJOR / MINOR / NONE

CONFESSIONS: MAJOR / MINOR / NONE

HOW WAS YOUR ENERGY?

MORNING: FULL TANK / HALF TANK / EMPTY   NOON: FULL TANK / HALF TANK / EMPTY

AFTERNOON: FULL TANK / HALF TANK / EMPTY

DID YOU NEED THE NURSE?

HEALTH: YES / NO   INJURY: YES / NO   PAIN: YES / NO

HOW WAS THE FOOD?

BREAKFAST: DELICIOUS / DECENT / DISGUSTING / DIDN'T EAT

LUNCH: DELICIOUS / DECENT / DISGUSTING / DIDN'T EAT

SNACKS: DELICIOUS / DECENT / DISGUSTING / DIDN'T EAT

QUIET   ANNOYED   COOL   SAD   TIRED   EXCITED   HAPPY   EMBARRASSED   SCARED

BORED   SICK   FRUSTRATED   ANGRY   FUNNY   PROUD   NERVOUS   GOOFY   SURPRISED

B = BEST PART OF YOUR DAY   W = WORST PART OF YOUR DAY   M = MOST OF THE DAY

RECORD IT
WHAT DID YOU LEARN TODAY?

MINIMUM FUNCTIONALITY

1) ABILITY	2) SKILL	3) VOCATION	4) RELATIONSHIP	5) MENTALITY
6) MENTAL EXERCISE	7) MUSCLE MEMORY	8) PRACTICE	9) TRAINING	10) EXPERIENCE

IN THIS CLASS	I ENGAGED MOST BY ...	MINIMUM FUNCTIONALITY	THIS CLASS	MAXIMUM POSSIBILITY
	THINKING SEEING LISTENING DOING			
	THINKING SEEING LISTENING DOING			
	THINKING SEEING LISTENING DOING			
	THINKING SEEING LISTENING DOING			
	THINKING SEEING LISTENING DOING			
	THINKING SEEING LISTENING DOING			
	THINKING SEEING LISTENING DOING			
	THINKING SEEING LISTENING DOING			

THIS INSTRUCTOR	BROUGHT ME THE MOST...
	EDUCATION
	TEACHING
	FUN
	CHALLENGES

THIS...	BROUGHT ME THE MOST ISSUES
CLASS	
CONCEPT	
LESSON	
INSTRUCTOR	

THIS CLASS	WAS THE MOST...
	EDUCATIONAL
	WORK
	FUN
	BORING

MAXIMUM POSSIBILITY

1) MOTIVATION	2) INSPIRATION	3) HIGHER EDUCATION	4) CAREER	5) DREAM
6) INVENTION	7) INNOVATION	8) NON-PROFIT	9) FORTUNE 500	10) SUPERHERO

HOW WAS SCHOOL TODAY?

DATE:_____

HOW DID YOU GET ALONG WITH PEOPLE?

ALLIES: POSITIVE / NEGATIVE / NEUTRAL

ANNOYANCES: POSITIVE / NEGATIVE / NEUTRAL   INSTRUCTORS: POSITIVE / NEGATIVE / NEUTRAL

HOW DID YOU BEHAVE?

SUCCESSES: MAJOR / MINOR / NONE

STRUGGLES: MAJOR / MINOR / NONE

CONFESSIONS: MAJOR / MINOR / NONE

HOW WAS YOUR ENERGY?

MORNING: FULL TANK / HALF TANK / EMPTY   NOON: FULL TANK / HALF TANK / EMPTY

AFTERNOON: FULL TANK / HALF TANK / EMPTY

DID YOU NEED THE NURSE?

HEALTH: YES / NO   INJURY: YES / NO   PAIN: YES / NO

HOW WAS THE FOOD?

BREAKFAST: DELICIOUS / DECENT / DISGUSTING / DIDN'T EAT

LUNCH: DELICIOUS / DECENT / DISGUSTING / DIDN'T EAT

SNACKS: DELICIOUS / DECENT / DISGUSTING / DIDN'T EAT

 QUIET
 ANNOYED
 COOL
 SAD
 TIRED
 EXCITED
 HAPPY
 EMBARRASSED
 SCARED

 BORED
 SICK
 FRUSTRATED
 ANGRY
 FUNNY
 PROUD
 NERVOUS
 GOOFY
 SURPRISED

B = BEST PART OF YOUR DAY   W = WORST PART OF YOUR DAY   M = MOST OF THE DAY

RECORD IT
WHAT DID YOU LEARN TODAY?

MINIMUM FUNCTIONALITY

1) ABILITY	2) SKILL	3) VOCATION	4) RELATIONSHIP	5) MENTALITY
6) MENTAL EXERCISE	7) MUSCLE MEMORY	8) PRACTICE	9) TRAINING	10) EXPERIENCE

IN THIS CLASS	I ENGAGED MOST BY ...	MINIMUM FUNCTIONALITY	THIS CLASS	MAXIMUM POSSIBILITY
	THINKING SEEING LISTENING DOING			
	THINKING SEEING LISTENING DOING			
	THINKING SEEING LISTENING DOING			
	THINKING SEEING LISTENING DOING			
	THINKING SEEING LISTENING DOING			
	THINKING SEEING LISTENING DOING			
	THINKING SEEING LISTENING DOING			
	THINKING SEEING LISTENING DOING			

THIS INSTRUCTOR	BROUGHT ME THE MOST...
	EDUCATION
	TEACHING
	FUN
	CHALLENGES

THIS...	BROUGHT ME THE MOST ISSUES
CLASS	
CONCEPT	
LESSON	
INSTRUCTOR	

THIS CLASS	WAS THE MOST...
	EDUCATIONAL
	WORK
	FUN
	BORING

MAXIMUM POSSIBILITY

1) MOTIVATION	2) INSPIRATION	3) HIGHER EDUCATION	4) CAREER	5) DREAM
6) INVENTION	7) INNOVATION	8) NON-PROFIT	9) FORTUNE 500	10) SUPERHERO

HOW WAS SCHOOL TODAY?

DATE:_____

HOW DID YOU GET ALONG WITH PEOPLE?

ALLIES: POSITIVE / NEGATIVE / NEUTRAL

ANNOYANCES: POSITIVE / NEGATIVE / NEUTRAL   INSTRUCTORS: POSITIVE / NEGATIVE / NEUTRAL

HOW DID YOU BEHAVE?

SUCCESSES: MAJOR / MINOR / NONE

STRUGGLES: MAJOR / MINOR / NONE

CONFESSIONS: MAJOR / MINOR / NONE

HOW WAS YOUR ENERGY?

MORNING: FULL TANK / HALF TANK / EMPTY   NOON: FULL TANK / HALF TANK / EMPTY

AFTERNOON: FULL TANK / HALF TANK / EMPTY

DID YOU NEED THE NURSE?

HEALTH: YES / NO   INJURY: YES / NO   PAIN: YES / NO

HOW WAS THE FOOD?

BREAKFAST: DELICIOUS / DECENT / DISGUSTING / DIDN'T EAT

LUNCH: DELICIOUS / DECENT / DISGUSTING / DIDN'T EAT

SNACKS: DELICIOUS / DECENT / DISGUSTING / DIDN'T EAT

QUIET   ANNOYED   COOL   SAD   TIRED   EXCITED   HAPPY   EMBARRASSED   SCARED

BORED   SICK   FRUSTRATED   ANGRY   FUNNY   PROUD   NERVOUS   GOOFY   SURPRISED

B = BEST PART OF YOUR DAY   W = WORST PART OF YOUR DAY   M = MOST OF THE DAY

RECORD IT
WHAT DID YOU LEARN TODAY?

MINIMUM FUNCTIONALITY

1) ABILITY	2) SKILL	3) VOCATION	4) RELATIONSHIP	5) MENTALITY
6) MENTAL EXERCISE	7) MUSCLE MEMORY	8) PRACTICE	9) TRAINING	10) EXPERIENCE

IN THIS CLASS	I ENGAGED MOST BY ...	MINIMUM FUNCTIONALITY	THIS CLASS	MAXIMUM POSSIBILITY
	THINKING SEEING LISTENING DOING			
	THINKING SEEING LISTENING DOING			
	THINKING SEEING LISTENING DOING			
	THINKING SEEING LISTENING DOING			
	THINKING SEEING LISTENING DOING			
	THINKING SEEING LISTENING DOING			
	THINKING SEEING LISTENING DOING			
	THINKING SEEING LISTENING DOING			

THIS INSTRUCTOR	BROUGHT ME THE MOST...
	EDUCATION
	TEACHING
	FUN
	CHALLENGES

THIS...	BROUGHT ME THE MOST ISSUES
CLASS	
CONCEPT	
LESSON	
INSTRUCTOR	

THIS CLASS	WAS THE MOST...
	EDUCATIONAL
	WORK
	FUN
	BORING

MAXIMUM POSSIBILITY

1) MOTIVATION	2) INSPIRATION	3) HIGHER EDUCATION	4) CAREER	5) DREAM
6) INVENTION	7) INNOVATION	8) NON-PROFIT	9) FORTUNE 500	10) SUPERHERO

HOW WAS SCHOOL TODAY?

DATE:_____

HOW DID YOU GET ALONG WITH PEOPLE?

ALLIES: POSITIVE / NEGATIVE / NEUTRAL

ANNOYANCES: POSITIVE / NEGATIVE / NEUTRAL   INSTRUCTORS: POSITIVE / NEGATIVE / NEUTRAL

HOW DID YOU BEHAVE?

SUCCESSES: MAJOR / MINOR / NONE

STRUGGLES: MAJOR / MINOR / NONE

CONFESSIONS: MAJOR / MINOR / NONE

HOW WAS YOUR ENERGY?

MORNING: FULL TANK / HALF TANK / EMPTY   NOON: FULL TANK / HALF TANK / EMPTY

AFTERNOON: FULL TANK / HALF TANK / EMPTY

DID YOU NEED THE NURSE?

HEALTH: YES / NO   INJURY: YES / NO   PAIN: YES / NO

HOW WAS THE FOOD?

BREAKFAST: DELICIOUS / DECENT / DISGUSTING / DIDN'T EAT

LUNCH: DELICIOUS / DECENT / DISGUSTING / DIDN'T EAT

SNACKS: DELICIOUS / DECENT / DISGUSTING / DIDN'T EAT

QUIET   ANNOYED   COOL   SAD   TIRED   EXCITED   HAPPY   EMBARRASSED   SCARED

BORED   SICK   FRUSTRATED   ANGRY   FUNNY   PROUD   NERVOUS   GOOFY   SURPRISED

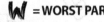 

B = BEST PART OF YOUR DAY   W = WORST PART OF YOUR DAY   M = MOST OF THE DAY

RECORD IT
WHAT DID YOU LEARN TODAY?

MINIMUM FUNCTIONALITY

| 1) ABILITY | 2) SKILL | 3) VOCATION | 4) RELATIONSHIP | 5) MENTALITY |
| 6) MENTAL EXERCISE | 7) MUSCLE MEMORY | 8) PRACTICE | 9) TRAINING | 10) EXPERIENCE |

IN THIS CLASS	I ENGAGED MOST BY ...	MINIMUM FUNCTIONALITY	THIS CLASS	MAXIMUM POSSIBILITY
	THINKING SEEING LISTENING DOING			
	THINKING SEEING LISTENING DOING			
	THINKING SEEING LISTENING DOING			
	THINKING SEEING LISTENING DOING			
	THINKING SEEING LISTENING DOING			
	THINKING SEEING LISTENING DOING			
	THINKING SEEING LISTENING DOING			
	THINKING SEEING LISTENING DOING			

THIS INSTRUCTOR	BROUGHT ME THE MOST...
	EDUCATION
	TEACHING
	FUN
	CHALLENGES

THIS...	BROUGHT ME THE MOST ISSUES
CLASS	
CONCEPT	
LESSON	
INSTRUCTOR	

THIS CLASS	WAS THE MOST...
	EDUCATIONAL
	WORK
	FUN
	BORING

MAXIMUM POSSIBILITY

| 1) MOTIVATION | 2) INSPIRATION | 3) HIGHER EDUCATION | 4) CAREER | 5) DREAM |
| 6) INVENTION | 7) INNOVATION | 8) NON-PROFIT | 9) FORTUNE 500 | 10) SUPERHERO |

HOW WAS SCHOOL TODAY?

DATE:_____

HOW DID YOU GET ALONG WITH PEOPLE?

ALLIES: POSITIVE / NEGATIVE / NEUTRAL

ANNOYANCES: POSITIVE / NEGATIVE / NEUTRAL   INSTRUCTORS: POSITIVE / NEGATIVE / NEUTRAL

HOW DID YOU BEHAVE?

SUCCESSES: MAJOR / MINOR / NONE

STRUGGLES: MAJOR / MINOR / NONE

CONFESSIONS: MAJOR / MINOR / NONE

HOW WAS YOUR ENERGY?

MORNING: FULL TANK / HALF TANK / EMPTY   NOON: FULL TANK / HALF TANK / EMPTY

AFTERNOON: FULL TANK / HALF TANK / EMPTY

DID YOU NEED THE NURSE?

HEALTH: YES / NO   INJURY: YES / NO   PAIN: YES / NO

HOW WAS THE FOOD?

BREAKFAST: DELICIOUS / DECENT / DISGUSTING / DIDN'T EAT

LUNCH: DELICIOUS / DECENT / DISGUSTING / DIDN'T EAT

SNACKS: DELICIOUS / DECENT / DISGUSTING / DIDN'T EAT

QUIET   ANNOYED   COOL   SAD   TIRED   EXCITED   HAPPY   EMBARRASSED   SCARED

BORED   SICK   FRUSTRATED   ANGRY   FUNNY   PROUD   NERVOUS   GOOFY   SURPRISED

B = BEST PART OF YOUR DAY   W = WORST PART OF YOUR DAY   M = MOST OF THE DAY

RECORD IT
WHAT DID YOU LEARN TODAY?

MINIMUM FUNCTIONALITY

1) ABILITY	2) SKILL	3) VOCATION	4) RELATIONSHIP	5) MENTALITY
6) MENTAL EXERCISE	7) MUSCLE MEMORY	8) PRACTICE	9) TRAINING	10) EXPERIENCE

IN THIS CLASS	I ENGAGED MOST BY ...	MINIMUM FUNCTIONALITY	THIS CLASS	MAXIMUM POSSIBILITY
	THINKING SEEING LISTENING DOING			
	THINKING SEEING LISTENING DOING			
	THINKING SEEING LISTENING DOING			
	THINKING SEEING LISTENING DOING			
	THINKING SEEING LISTENING DOING			
	THINKING SEEING LISTENING DOING			
	THINKING SEEING LISTENING DOING			
	THINKING SEEING LISTENING DOING			

THIS INSTRUCTOR	BROUGHT ME THE MOST...
	EDUCATION
	TEACHING
	FUN
	CHALLENGES

THIS...	BROUGHT ME THE MOST ISSUES
CLASS	
CONCEPT	
LESSON	
INSTRUCTOR	

THIS CLASS	WAS THE MOST...
	EDUCATIONAL
	WORK
	FUN
	BORING

MAXIMUM POSSIBILITY

1) MOTIVATION	2) INSPIRATION	3) HIGHER EDUCATION	4) CAREER	5) DREAM
6) INVENTION	7) INNOVATION	8) NON-PROFIT	9) FORTUNE 500	10) SUPERHERO

How Was School Today?

DATE:_____

HOW DID YOU GET ALONG WITH PEOPLE?

ALLIES: POSITIVE / NEGATIVE / NEUTRAL

ANNOYANCES: POSITIVE / NEGATIVE / NEUTRAL   INSTRUCTORS: POSITIVE / NEGATIVE / NEUTRAL

HOW DID YOU BEHAVE?

SUCCESSES: MAJOR / MINOR / NONE

STRUGGLES: MAJOR / MINOR / NONE

CONFESSIONS: MAJOR / MINOR / NONE

HOW WAS YOUR ENERGY?

MORNING: FULL TANK / HALF TANK / EMPTY   NOON: FULL TANK / HALF TANK / EMPTY

AFTERNOON: FULL TANK / HALF TANK / EMPTY

DID YOU NEED THE NURSE?

HEALTH: YES / NO   INJURY: YES / NO   PAIN: YES / NO

HOW WAS THE FOOD?

BREAKFAST: DELICIOUS / DECENT / DISGUSTING / DIDN'T EAT

LUNCH: DELICIOUS / DECENT / DISGUSTING / DIDN'T EAT

SNACKS: DELICIOUS / DECENT / DISGUSTING / DIDN'T EAT

QUIET   ANNOYED   COOL   SAD   TIRED   EXCITED   HAPPY   EMBARRASSED   SCARED

BORED   SICK   FRUSTRATED   ANGRY   FUNNY   PROUD   NERVOUS   GOOFY   SURPRISED

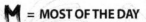

B = BEST PART OF YOUR DAY   **W** = WORST PART OF YOUR DAY   **M** = MOST OF THE DAY

RECORD IT
WHAT DID YOU LEARN TODAY?

MINIMUM FUNCTIONALITY

1) ABILITY	2) SKILL	3) VOCATION	4) RELATIONSHIP	5) MENTALITY
6) MENTAL EXERCISE	7) MUSCLE MEMORY	8) PRACTICE	9) TRAINING	10) EXPERIENCE

IN THIS CLASS	I ENGAGED MOST BY ...	MINIMUM FUNCTIONALITY	THIS CLASS	MAXIMUM POSSIBILITY
	THINKING SEEING LISTENING DOING			
	THINKING SEEING LISTENING DOING			
	THINKING SEEING LISTENING DOING			
	THINKING SEEING LISTENING DOING			
	THINKING SEEING LISTENING DOING			
	THINKING SEEING LISTENING DOING			
	THINKING SEEING LISTENING DOING			
	THINKING SEEING LISTENING DOING			

THIS INSTRUCTOR	BROUGHT ME THE MOST...
	EDUCATION
	TEACHING
	FUN
	CHALLENGES

THIS...	BROUGHT ME THE MOST ISSUES
CLASS	
CONCEPT	
LESSON	
INSTRUCTOR	

THIS CLASS	WAS THE MOST...
	EDUCATIONAL
	WORK
	FUN
	BORING

MAXIMUM POSSIBILITY

1) MOTIVATION	2) INSPIRATION	3) HIGHER EDUCATION	4) CAREER	5) DREAM
6) INVENTION	7) INNOVATION	8) NON-PROFIT	9) FORTUNE 500	10) SUPERHERO

RECORD IT
HOW WAS SCHOOL TODAY?

DATE: _____

HOW DID YOU GET ALONG WITH PEOPLE?

ALLIES: POSITIVE / NEGATIVE / NEUTRAL

ANNOYANCES: POSITIVE / NEGATIVE / NEUTRAL   INSTRUCTORS: POSITIVE / NEGATIVE / NEUTRAL

HOW DID YOU BEHAVE?

SUCCESSES: MAJOR / MINOR / NONE

STRUGGLES: MAJOR / MINOR / NONE

CONFESSIONS: MAJOR / MINOR / NONE

HOW WAS YOUR ENERGY?

MORNING: FULL TANK / HALF TANK / EMPTY   NOON: FULL TANK / HALF TANK / EMPTY

AFTERNOON: FULL TANK / HALF TANK / EMPTY

DID YOU NEED THE NURSE?

HEALTH: YES / NO   INJURY: YES / NO   PAIN: YES / NO

HOW WAS THE FOOD?

BREAKFAST: DELICIOUS / DECENT / DISGUSTING / DIDN'T EAT

LUNCH: DELICIOUS / DECENT / DISGUSTING / DIDN'T EAT

SNACKS: DELICIOUS / DECENT / DISGUSTING / DIDN'T EAT

QUIET   ANNOYED   COOL   SAD   TIRED   EXCITED   HAPPY   EMBARRASSED   SCARED

BORED   SICK   FRUSTRATED   ANGRY   FUNNY   PROUD   NERVOUS   GOOFY   SURPRISED

B = BEST PART OF YOUR DAY   **W** = WORST PART OF YOUR DAY   **M** = MOST OF THE DAY

RECORD IT
WHAT DID YOU LEARN TODAY?

MINIMUM FUNCTIONALITY

1) ABILITY	2) SKILL	3) VOCATION	4) RELATIONSHIP	5) MENTALITY
6) MENTAL EXERCISE	7) MUSCLE MEMORY	8) PRACTICE	9) TRAINING	10) EXPERIENCE

IN THIS CLASS	I ENGAGED MOST BY ...	MINIMUM FUNCTIONALITY	THIS CLASS	MAXIMUM POSSIBILITY
	THINKING SEEING LISTENING DOING			
	THINKING SEEING LISTENING DOING			
	THINKING SEEING LISTENING DOING			
	THINKING SEEING LISTENING DOING			
	THINKING SEEING LISTENING DOING			
	THINKING SEEING LISTENING DOING			
	THINKING SEEING LISTENING DOING			
	THINKING SEEING LISTENING DOING			

THIS INSTRUCTOR	BROUGHT ME THE MOST...
	EDUCATION
	TEACHING
	FUN
	CHALLENGES

THIS...	BROUGHT ME THE MOST ISSUES
CLASS	
CONCEPT	
LESSON	
INSTRUCTOR	

THIS CLASS	WAS THE MOST...
	EDUCATIONAL
	WORK
	FUN
	BORING

MAXIMUM POSSIBILITY

1) MOTIVATION	2) INSPIRATION	3) HIGHER EDUCATION	4) CAREER	5) DREAM
6) INVENTION	7) INNOVATION	8) NON-PROFIT	9) FORTUNE 500	10) SUPERHERO

RECORD IT
HOW WAS SCHOOL TODAY?

DATE:_____

HOW DID YOU GET ALONG WITH PEOPLE?

ALLIES: POSITIVE / NEGATIVE / NEUTRAL

ANNOYANCES: POSITIVE / NEGATIVE / NEUTRAL   INSTRUCTORS: POSITIVE / NEGATIVE / NEUTRAL

HOW DID YOU BEHAVE?

SUCCESSES: MAJOR / MINOR / NONE

STRUGGLES: MAJOR / MINOR / NONE

CONFESSIONS: MAJOR / MINOR / NONE

HOW WAS YOUR ENERGY?

MORNING: FULL TANK / HALF TANK / EMPTY   NOON: FULL TANK / HALF TANK / EMPTY

AFTERNOON: FULL TANK / HALF TANK / EMPTY

DID YOU NEED THE NURSE?

HEALTH: YES / NO   INJURY: YES / NO   PAIN: YES / NO

HOW WAS THE FOOD?

BREAKFAST: DELICIOUS / DECENT / DISGUSTING / DIDN'T EAT

LUNCH: DELICIOUS / DECENT / DISGUSTING / DIDN'T EAT

SNACKS: DELICIOUS / DECENT / DISGUSTING / DIDN'T EAT

QUIET   ANNOYED   COOL   SAD   TIRED   EXCITED   HAPPY   EMBARRASSED   SCARED

BORED   SICK   FRUSTRATED   ANGRY   FUNNY   PROUD   NERVOUS   GOOFY   SURPRISED

B = BEST PART OF YOUR DAY   **W** = WORST PART OF YOUR DAY   **M** = MOST OF THE DAY

RECORD IT
WHAT DID YOU LEARN TODAY?

MINIMUM FUNCTIONALITY

1) ABILITY	2) SKILL	3) VOCATION	4) RELATIONSHIP	5) MENTALITY
6) MENTAL EXERCISE	7) MUSCLE MEMORY	8) PRACTICE	9) TRAINING	10) EXPERIENCE

IN THIS CLASS	I ENGAGED MOST BY ...	MINIMUM FUNCTIONALITY	THIS CLASS	MAXIMUM POSSIBILITY
	THINKING SEEING LISTENING DOING			
	THINKING SEEING LISTENING DOING			
	THINKING SEEING LISTENING DOING			
	THINKING SEEING LISTENING DOING			
	THINKING SEEING LISTENING DOING			
	THINKING SEEING LISTENING DOING			
	THINKING SEEING LISTENING DOING			
	THINKING SEEING LISTENING DOING			

THIS INSTRUCTOR	BROUGHT ME THE MOST...
	EDUCATION
	TEACHING
	FUN
	CHALLENGES

THIS...	BROUGHT ME THE MOST ISSUES
CLASS	
CONCEPT	
LESSON	
INSTRUCTOR	

THIS CLASS	WAS THE MOST...
	EDUCATIONAL
	WORK
	FUN
	BORING

MAXIMUM POSSIBILITY

1) MOTIVATION	2) INSPIRATION	3) HIGHER EDUCATION	4) CAREER	5) DREAM
6) INVENTION	7) INNOVATION	8) NON-PROFIT	9) FORTUNE 500	10) SUPERHERO

RECORD IT
HOW WAS SCHOOL TODAY?

DATE:_____

HOW DID YOU GET ALONG WITH PEOPLE?

ALLIES: POSITIVE / NEGATIVE / NEUTRAL

ANNOYANCES: POSITIVE / NEGATIVE / NEUTRAL   INSTRUCTORS: POSITIVE / NEGATIVE / NEUTRAL

HOW DID YOU BEHAVE?

SUCCESSES: MAJOR / MINOR / NONE

STRUGGLES: MAJOR / MINOR / NONE

CONFESSIONS: MAJOR / MINOR / NONE

HOW WAS YOUR ENERGY?

MORNING: FULL TANK / HALF TANK / EMPTY   NOON: FULL TANK / HALF TANK / EMPTY

AFTERNOON: FULL TANK / HALF TANK / EMPTY

DID YOU NEED THE NURSE?

HEALTH: YES / NO   INJURY: YES / NO   PAIN: YES / NO

HOW WAS THE FOOD?

BREAKFAST: DELICIOUS / DECENT / DISGUSTING / DIDN'T EAT

LUNCH: DELICIOUS / DECENT / DISGUSTING / DIDN'T EAT

SNACKS: DELICIOUS / DECENT / DISGUSTING / DIDN'T EAT

QUIET   ANNOYED   COOL   SAD   TIRED   EXCITED   HAPPY   EMBARRASSED   SCARED

BORED   SICK   FRUSTRATED   ANGRY   FUNNY   PROUD   NERVOUS   GOOFY   SURPRISED

B = BEST PART OF YOUR DAY   **W** = WORST PART OF YOUR DAY   **M** = MOST OF THE DAY

RECORD IT
WHAT DID YOU LEARN TODAY?

MINIMUM FUNCTIONALITY

1) ABILITY	2) SKILL	3) VOCATION	4) RELATIONSHIP	5) MENTALITY
6) MENTAL EXERCISE	7) MUSCLE MEMORY	8) PRACTICE	9) TRAINING	10) EXPERIENCE

IN THIS CLASS	I ENGAGED MOST BY ...	MINIMUM FUNCTIONALITY	THIS CLASS	MAXIMUM POSSIBILITY
	THINKING SEEING LISTENING DOING			
	THINKING SEEING LISTENING DOING			
	THINKING SEEING LISTENING DOING			
	THINKING SEEING LISTENING DOING			
	THINKING SEEING LISTENING DOING			
	THINKING SEEING LISTENING DOING			
	THINKING SEEING LISTENING DOING			
	THINKING SEEING LISTENING DOING			

THIS INSTRUCTOR	BROUGHT ME THE MOST...
	EDUCATION
	TEACHING
	FUN
	CHALLENGES

THIS...	BROUGHT ME THE MOST ISSUES
CLASS	
CONCEPT	
LESSON	
INSTRUCTOR	

THIS CLASS	WAS THE MOST...
	EDUCATIONAL
	WORK
	FUN
	BORING

MAXIMUM POSSIBILITY

1) MOTIVATION	2) INSPIRATION	3) HIGHER EDUCATION	4) CAREER	5) DREAM
6) INVENTION	7) INNOVATION	8) NON-PROFIT	9) FORTUNE 500	10) SUPERHERO

RECORD IT
How Was School Today?

DATE:_____

HOW DID YOU GET ALONG WITH PEOPLE?

ALLIES: POSITIVE / NEGATIVE / NEUTRAL

ANNOYANCES: POSITIVE / NEGATIVE / NEUTRAL   INSTRUCTORS: POSITIVE / NEGATIVE / NEUTRAL

HOW DID YOU BEHAVE?

SUCCESSES: MAJOR / MINOR / NONE

STRUGGLES: MAJOR / MINOR / NONE

CONFESSIONS: MAJOR / MINOR / NONE

HOW WAS YOUR ENERGY?

MORNING: FULL TANK / HALF TANK / EMPTY   NOON: FULL TANK / HALF TANK / EMPTY

AFTERNOON: FULL TANK / HALF TANK / EMPTY

DID YOU NEED THE NURSE?

HEALTH: YES / NO   INJURY: YES / NO   PAIN: YES / NO

HOW WAS THE FOOD?

BREAKFAST: DELICIOUS / DECENT / DISGUSTING / DIDN'T EAT

LUNCH: DELICIOUS / DECENT / DISGUSTING / DIDN'T EAT

SNACKS: DELICIOUS / DECENT / DISGUSTING / DIDN'T EAT

QUIET   ANNOYED   COOL   SAD   TIRED   EXCITED   HAPPY   EMBARRASSED   SCARED

BORED   SICK   FRUSTRATED   ANGRY   FUNNY   PROUD   NERVOUS   GOOFY   SURPRISED

B = BEST PART OF YOUR DAY   W = WORST PART OF YOUR DAY   M = MOST OF THE DAY

RECORD IT
WHAT DID YOU LEARN TODAY?

MINIMUM FUNCTIONALITY

1) ABILITY	2) SKILL	3) VOCATION	4) RELATIONSHIP	5) MENTALITY
6) MENTAL EXERCISE	7) MUSCLE MEMORY	8) PRACTICE	9) TRAINING	10) EXPERIENCE

IN THIS CLASS	I ENGAGED MOST BY ...	MINIMUM FUNCTIONALITY	THIS CLASS	MAXIMUM POSSIBILITY
	THINKING SEEING LISTENING DOING			
	THINKING SEEING LISTENING DOING			
	THINKING SEEING LISTENING DOING			
	THINKING SEEING LISTENING DOING			
	THINKING SEEING LISTENING DOING			
	THINKING SEEING LISTENING DOING			
	THINKING SEEING LISTENING DOING			
	THINKING SEEING LISTENING DOING			

THIS INSTRUCTOR	BROUGHT ME THE MOST...
	EDUCATION
	TEACHING
	FUN
	CHALLENGES

THIS...	BROUGHT ME THE MOST ISSUES
CLASS	
CONCEPT	
LESSON	
INSTRUCTOR	

THIS CLASS	WAS THE MOST...
	EDUCATIONAL
	WORK
	FUN
	BORING

MAXIMUM POSSIBILITY

1) MOTIVATION	2) INSPIRATION	3) HIGHER EDUCATION	4) CAREER	5) DREAM
6) INVENTION	7) INNOVATION	8) NON-PROFIT	9) FORTUNE 500	10) SUPERHERO

HOW WAS SCHOOL TODAY?

DATE:_____

HOW DID YOU GET ALONG WITH PEOPLE?

ALLIES: POSITIVE / NEGATIVE / NEUTRAL

ANNOYANCES: POSITIVE / NEGATIVE / NEUTRAL   INSTRUCTORS: POSITIVE / NEGATIVE / NEUTRAL

HOW DID YOU BEHAVE?

SUCCESSES: MAJOR / MINOR / NONE

STRUGGLES: MAJOR / MINOR / NONE

CONFESSIONS: MAJOR / MINOR / NONE

HOW WAS YOUR ENERGY?

MORNING: FULL TANK / HALF TANK / EMPTY   NOON: FULL TANK / HALF TANK / EMPTY

AFTERNOON: FULL TANK / HALF TANK / EMPTY

DID YOU NEED THE NURSE?

HEALTH: YES / NO   INJURY: YES / NO   PAIN: YES / NO

HOW WAS THE FOOD?

BREAKFAST: DELICIOUS / DECENT / DISGUSTING / DIDN'T EAT

LUNCH: DELICIOUS / DECENT / DISGUSTING / DIDN'T EAT

SNACKS: DELICIOUS / DECENT / DISGUSTING / DIDN'T EAT

QUIET   ANNOYED   COOL   SAD   TIRED   EXCITED   HAPPY   EMBARRASSED   SCARED

BORED   SICK   FRUSTRATED   ANGRY   FUNNY   PROUD   NERVOUS   GOOFY   SURPRISED

B = BEST PART OF YOUR DAY   W = WORST PART OF YOUR DAY   M = MOST OF THE DAY

RECORD IT
WHAT DID YOU LEARN TODAY?

MINIMUM FUNCTIONALITY

1) ABILITY	2) SKILL	3) VOCATION	4) RELATIONSHIP	5) MENTALITY
6) MENTAL EXERCISE	7) MUSCLE MEMORY	8) PRACTICE	9) TRAINING	10) EXPERIENCE

IN THIS CLASS	I ENGAGED MOST BY ...	MINIMUM FUNCTIONALITY	THIS CLASS	MAXIMUM POSSIBILITY
	THINKING SEEING LISTENING DOING			
	THINKING SEEING LISTENING DOING			
	THINKING SEEING LISTENING DOING			
	THINKING SEEING LISTENING DOING			
	THINKING SEEING LISTENING DOING			
	THINKING SEEING LISTENING DOING			
	THINKING SEEING LISTENING DOING			
	THINKING SEEING LISTENING DOING			

THIS INSTRUCTOR	BROUGHT ME THE MOST...
	EDUCATION
	TEACHING
	FUN
	CHALLENGES

THIS...	BROUGHT ME THE MOST ISSUES
CLASS	
CONCEPT	
LESSON	
INSTRUCTOR	

THIS CLASS	WAS THE MOST...
	EDUCATIONAL
	WORK
	FUN
	BORING

MAXIMUM POSSIBILITY

1) MOTIVATION	2) INSPIRATION	3) HIGHER EDUCATION	4) CAREER	5) DREAM
6) INVENTION	7) INNOVATION	8) NON-PROFIT	9) FORTUNE 500	10) SUPERHERO

RECORD IT
HOW WAS SCHOOL TODAY?

DATE:_____

HOW DID YOU GET ALONG WITH PEOPLE?

ALLIES: POSITIVE / NEGATIVE / NEUTRAL

ANNOYANCES: POSITIVE / NEGATIVE / NEUTRAL   INSTRUCTORS: POSITIVE / NEGATIVE / NEUTRAL

HOW DID YOU BEHAVE?

SUCCESSES: MAJOR / MINOR / NONE

STRUGGLES: MAJOR / MINOR / NONE

CONFESSIONS: MAJOR / MINOR / NONE

HOW WAS YOUR ENERGY?

MORNING: FULL TANK / HALF TANK / EMPTY   NOON: FULL TANK / HALF TANK / EMPTY

AFTERNOON: FULL TANK / HALF TANK / EMPTY

DID YOU NEED THE NURSE?

HEALTH: YES / NO   INJURY: YES / NO   PAIN: YES / NO

HOW WAS THE FOOD?

BREAKFAST: DELICIOUS / DECENT / DISGUSTING / DIDN'T EAT

LUNCH: DELICIOUS / DECENT / DISGUSTING / DIDN'T EAT

SNACKS: DELICIOUS / DECENT / DISGUSTING / DIDN'T EAT

QUIET   ANNOYED   COOL   SAD   TIRED   EXCITED   HAPPY   EMBARRASSED   SCARED

BORED   SICK   FRUSTRATED   ANGRY   FUNNY   PROUD   NERVOUS   GOOFY   SURPRISED

B = BEST PART OF YOUR DAY   **W** = WORST PART OF YOUR DAY   **M** = MOST OF THE DAY

RECORD IT
WHAT DID YOU LEARN TODAY?

MINIMUM FUNCTIONALITY

1) ABILITY	2) SKILL	3) VOCATION	4) RELATIONSHIP	5) MENTALITY
6) MENTAL EXERCISE	7) MUSCLE MEMORY	8) PRACTICE	9) TRAINING	10) EXPERIENCE

IN THIS CLASS	I ENGAGED MOST BY ...
	THINKING SEEING LISTENING DOING
	THINKING SEEING LISTENING DOING
	THINKING SEEING LISTENING DOING
	THINKING SEEING LISTENING DOING
	THINKING SEEING LISTENING DOING
	THINKING SEEING LISTENING DOING
	THINKING SEEING LISTENING DOING
	THINKING SEEING LISTENING DOING

MINIMUM FUNCTIONALITY	THIS CLASS	MAXIMUM POSSIBILITY

THIS INSTRUCTOR	BROUGHT ME THE MOST...
	EDUCATION
	TEACHING
	FUN
	CHALLENGES

THIS...	BROUGHT ME THE MOST ISSUES
CLASS	
CONCEPT	
LESSON	
INSTRUCTOR	

THIS CLASS	WAS THE MOST...
	EDUCATIONAL
	WORK
	FUN
	BORING

MAXIMUM POSSIBILITY

1) MOTIVATION	2) INSPIRATION	3) HIGHER EDUCATION	4) CAREER	5) DREAM
6) INVENTION	7) INNOVATION	8) NON-PROFIT	9) FORTUNE 500	10) SUPERHERO

How Was School Today?

DATE:_____

HOW DID YOU GET ALONG WITH PEOPLE?

ALLIES: POSITIVE / NEGATIVE / NEUTRAL

ANNOYANCES: POSITIVE / NEGATIVE / NEUTRAL   INSTRUCTORS: POSITIVE / NEGATIVE / NEUTRAL

HOW DID YOU BEHAVE?

SUCCESSES: MAJOR / MINOR / NONE

STRUGGLES: MAJOR / MINOR / NONE

CONFESSIONS: MAJOR / MINOR / NONE

HOW WAS YOUR ENERGY?

MORNING: FULL TANK / HALF TANK / EMPTY   NOON: FULL TANK / HALF TANK / EMPTY

AFTERNOON: FULL TANK / HALF TANK / EMPTY

DID YOU NEED THE NURSE?

HEALTH: YES / NO   INJURY: YES / NO   PAIN: YES / NO

HOW WAS THE FOOD?

BREAKFAST: DELICIOUS / DECENT / DISGUSTING / DIDN'T EAT

LUNCH: DELICIOUS / DECENT / DISGUSTING / DIDN'T EAT

SNACKS: DELICIOUS / DECENT / DISGUSTING / DIDN'T EAT

QUIET   ANNOYED   COOL   SAD   TIRED   EXCITED   HAPPY   EMBARRASSED   SCARED

BORED   SICK   FRUSTRATED   ANGRY   FUNNY   PROUD   NERVOUS   GOOFY   SURPRISED

B = BEST PART OF YOUR DAY   W = WORST PART OF YOUR DAY   M = MOST OF THE DAY

RECORD IT
WHAT DID YOU LEARN TODAY?

MINIMUM FUNCTIONALITY

| 1) ABILITY | 2) SKILL | 3) VOCATION | 4) RELATIONSHIP | 5) MENTALITY |
| 6) MENTAL EXERCISE | 7) MUSCLE MEMORY | 8) PRACTICE | 9) TRAINING | 10) EXPERIENCE |

IN THIS CLASS	I ENGAGED MOST BY …	MINIMUM FUNCTIONALITY	THIS CLASS	MAXIMUM POSSIBILITY
	THINKING SEEING LISTENING DOING			
	THINKING SEEING LISTENING DOING			
	THINKING SEEING LISTENING DOING			
	THINKING SEEING LISTENING DOING			
	THINKING SEEING LISTENING DOING			
	THINKING SEEING LISTENING DOING			
	THINKING SEEING LISTENING DOING			
	THINKING SEEING LISTENING DOING			

THIS INSTRUCTOR	BROUGHT ME THE MOST…
	EDUCATION
	TEACHING
	FUN
	CHALLENGES

THIS…	BROUGHT ME THE MOST ISSUES
CLASS	
CONCEPT	
LESSON	
INSTRUCTOR	

THIS CLASS	WAS THE MOST…
	EDUCATIONAL
	WORK
	FUN
	BORING

MAXIMUM POSSIBILITY

| 1) MOTIVATION | 2) INSPIRATION | 3) HIGHER EDUCATION | 4) CAREER | 5) DREAM |
| 6) INVENTION | 7) INNOVATION | 8) NON-PROFIT | 9) FORTUNE 500 | 10) SUPERHERO |

RECORD IT
HOW WAS SCHOOL TODAY?

DATE:_____

HOW DID YOU GET ALONG WITH PEOPLE?

ALLIES: POSITIVE / NEGATIVE / NEUTRAL

ANNOYANCES: POSITIVE / NEGATIVE / NEUTRAL   INSTRUCTORS: POSITIVE / NEGATIVE / NEUTRAL

HOW DID YOU BEHAVE?

SUCCESSES: MAJOR / MINOR / NONE

STRUGGLES: MAJOR / MINOR / NONE

CONFESSIONS: MAJOR / MINOR / NONE

HOW WAS YOUR ENERGY?

MORNING: FULL TANK / HALF TANK / EMPTY   NOON: FULL TANK / HALF TANK / EMPTY

AFTERNOON: FULL TANK / HALF TANK / EMPTY

DID YOU NEED THE NURSE?

HEALTH: YES / NO   INJURY: YES / NO   PAIN: YES / NO

HOW WAS THE FOOD?

BREAKFAST: DELICIOUS / DECENT / DISGUSTING / DIDN'T EAT

LUNCH: DELICIOUS / DECENT / DISGUSTING / DIDN'T EAT

SNACKS: DELICIOUS / DECENT / DISGUSTING / DIDN'T EAT

QUIET   ANNOYED   COOL   SAD   TIRED   EXCITED   HAPPY   EMBARRASSED   SCARED

BORED   SICK   FRUSTRATED   ANGRY   FUNNY   PROUD   NERVOUS   GOOFY   SURPRISED

B = BEST PART OF YOUR DAY   W = WORST PART OF YOUR DAY   M = MOST OF THE DAY

RECORD IT
WHAT DID YOU LEARN TODAY?

MINIMUM FUNCTIONALITY

1) ABILITY	2) SKILL	3) VOCATION	4) RELATIONSHIP	5) MENTALITY
6) MENTAL EXERCISE	7) MUSCLE MEMORY	8) PRACTICE	9) TRAINING	10) EXPERIENCE

IN THIS CLASS	I ENGAGED MOST BY ...	MINIMUM FUNCTIONALITY	THIS CLASS	MAXIMUM POSSIBILITY
	THINKING SEEING LISTENING DOING			
	THINKING SEEING LISTENING DOING			
	THINKING SEEING LISTENING DOING			
	THINKING SEEING LISTENING DOING			
	THINKING SEEING LISTENING DOING			
	THINKING SEEING LISTENING DOING			
	THINKING SEEING LISTENING DOING			
	THINKING SEEING LISTENING DOING			

THIS INSTRUCTOR	BROUGHT ME THE MOST...
	EDUCATION
	TEACHING
	FUN
	CHALLENGES

THIS...	BROUGHT ME THE MOST ISSUES
CLASS	
CONCEPT	
LESSON	
INSTRUCTOR	

THIS CLASS	WAS THE MOST...
	EDUCATIONAL
	WORK
	FUN
	BORING

MAXIMUM POSSIBILITY

1) MOTIVATION	2) INSPIRATION	3) HIGHER EDUCATION	4) CAREER	5) DREAM
6) INVENTION	7) INNOVATION	8) NON-PROFIT	9) FORTUNE 500	10) SUPERHERO

RECORD IT
HOW WAS SCHOOL TODAY?

DATE:_____

HOW DID YOU GET ALONG WITH PEOPLE?

ALLIES: POSITIVE / NEGATIVE / NEUTRAL

ANNOYANCES: POSITIVE / NEGATIVE / NEUTRAL   INSTRUCTORS: POSITIVE / NEGATIVE / NEUTRAL

HOW DID YOU BEHAVE?

SUCCESSES: MAJOR / MINOR / NONE

STRUGGLES: MAJOR / MINOR / NONE

CONFESSIONS: MAJOR / MINOR / NONE

HOW WAS YOUR ENERGY?

MORNING: FULL TANK / HALF TANK / EMPTY   NOON: FULL TANK / HALF TANK / EMPTY

AFTERNOON: FULL TANK / HALF TANK / EMPTY

DID YOU NEED THE NURSE?

HEALTH: YES / NO   INJURY: YES / NO   PAIN: YES / NO

HOW WAS THE FOOD?

BREAKFAST: DELICIOUS / DECENT / DISGUSTING / DIDN'T EAT

LUNCH: DELICIOUS / DECENT / DISGUSTING / DIDN'T EAT

SNACKS: DELICIOUS / DECENT / DISGUSTING / DIDN'T EAT

QUIET   ANNOYED   COOL   SAD   TIRED   EXCITED   HAPPY   EMBARRASSED   SCARED

BORED   SICK   FRUSTRATED   ANGRY   FUNNY   PROUD   NERVOUS   GOOFY   SURPRISED

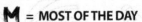

B = BEST PART OF YOUR DAY   **W** = WORST PART OF YOUR DAY   **M** = MOST OF THE DAY

RECORD IT
WHAT DID YOU LEARN TODAY?

MINIMUM FUNCTIONALITY

1) ABILITY	2) SKILL	3) VOCATION	4) RELATIONSHIP	5) MENTALITY
6) MENTAL EXERCISE	7) MUSCLE MEMORY	8) PRACTICE	9) TRAINING	10) EXPERIENCE

IN THIS CLASS	I ENGAGED MOST BY ...	MINIMUM FUNCTIONALITY	THIS CLASS	MAXIMUM POSSIBILITY
	THINKING SEEING LISTENING DOING			
	THINKING SEEING LISTENING DOING			
	THINKING SEEING LISTENING DOING			
	THINKING SEEING LISTENING DOING			
	THINKING SEEING LISTENING DOING			
	THINKING SEEING LISTENING DOING			
	THINKING SEEING LISTENING DOING			
	THINKING SEEING LISTENING DOING			

THIS INSTRUCTOR	BROUGHT ME THE MOST...
	EDUCATION
	TEACHING
	FUN
	CHALLENGES

THIS...	BROUGHT ME THE MOST ISSUES
CLASS	
CONCEPT	
LESSON	
INSTRUCTOR	

THIS CLASS	WAS THE MOST...
	EDUCATIONAL
	WORK
	FUN
	BORING

MAXIMUM POSSIBILITY

1) MOTIVATION	2) INSPIRATION	3) HIGHER EDUCATION	4) CAREER	5) DREAM
6) INVENTION	7) INNOVATION	8) NON-PROFIT	9) FORTUNE 500	10) SUPERHERO

HOW WAS SCHOOL TODAY?

DATE: _____

HOW DID YOU GET ALONG WITH PEOPLE?

ALLIES: POSITIVE / NEGATIVE / NEUTRAL

ANNOYANCES: POSITIVE / NEGATIVE / NEUTRAL   INSTRUCTORS: POSITIVE / NEGATIVE / NEUTRAL

HOW DID YOU BEHAVE?

SUCCESSES: MAJOR / MINOR / NONE

STRUGGLES: MAJOR / MINOR / NONE

CONFESSIONS: MAJOR / MINOR / NONE

HOW WAS YOUR ENERGY?

MORNING: FULL TANK / HALF TANK / EMPTY   NOON: FULL TANK / HALF TANK / EMPTY

AFTERNOON: FULL TANK / HALF TANK / EMPTY

DID YOU NEED THE NURSE?

HEALTH: YES / NO   INJURY: YES / NO   PAIN: YES / NO

HOW WAS THE FOOD?

BREAKFAST: DELICIOUS / DECENT / DISGUSTING / DIDN'T EAT

LUNCH: DELICIOUS / DECENT / DISGUSTING / DIDN'T EAT

SNACKS: DELICIOUS / DECENT / DISGUSTING / DIDN'T EAT

QUIET   ANNOYED   COOL   SAD   TIRED   EXCITED   HAPPY   EMBARRASSED   SCARED

BORED   SICK   FRUSTRATED   ANGRY   FUNNY   PROUD   NERVOUS   GOOFY   SURPRISED

B = BEST PART OF YOUR DAY   **W** = WORST PART OF YOUR DAY   **M** = MOST OF THE DAY

RECORD IT
WHAT DID YOU LEARN TODAY?

MINIMUM FUNCTIONALITY

1) ABILITY	2) SKILL	3) VOCATION	4) RELATIONSHIP	5) MENTALITY
6) MENTAL EXERCISE	7) MUSCLE MEMORY	8) PRACTICE	9) TRAINING	10) EXPERIENCE

IN THIS CLASS	I ENGAGED MOST BY ...
	THINKING SEEING LISTENING DOING
	THINKING SEEING LISTENING DOING
	THINKING SEEING LISTENING DOING
	THINKING SEEING LISTENING DOING
	THINKING SEEING LISTENING DOING
	THINKING SEEING LISTENING DOING
	THINKING SEEING LISTENING DOING
	THINKING SEEING LISTENING DOING

MINIMUM FUNCTIONALITY	THIS CLASS	MAXIMUM POSSIBILITY

THIS INSTRUCTOR	BROUGHT ME THE MOST...
	EDUCATION
	TEACHING
	FUN
	CHALLENGES

THIS...	BROUGHT ME THE MOST ISSUES
CLASS	
CONCEPT	
LESSON	
INSTRUCTOR	

THIS CLASS	WAS THE MOST...
	EDUCATIONAL
	WORK
	FUN
	BORING

MAXIMUM POSSIBILITY

1) MOTIVATION	2) INSPIRATION	3) HIGHER EDUCATION	4) CAREER	5) DREAM
6) INVENTION	7) INNOVATION	8) NON-PROFIT	9) FORTUNE 500	10) SUPERHERO

RECORD IT
HOW WAS SCHOOL TODAY?

DATE:_____

HOW DID YOU GET ALONG WITH PEOPLE?

ALLIES: POSITIVE / NEGATIVE / NEUTRAL

ANNOYANCES: POSITIVE / NEGATIVE / NEUTRAL   INSTRUCTORS: POSITIVE / NEGATIVE / NEUTRAL

HOW DID YOU BEHAVE?

SUCCESSES: MAJOR / MINOR / NONE

STRUGGLES: MAJOR / MINOR / NONE

CONFESSIONS: MAJOR / MINOR / NONE

HOW WAS YOUR ENERGY?

MORNING: FULL TANK / HALF TANK / EMPTY   NOON: FULL TANK / HALF TANK / EMPTY

AFTERNOON: FULL TANK / HALF TANK / EMPTY

DID YOU NEED THE NURSE?

HEALTH: YES / NO   INJURY: YES / NO   PAIN: YES / NO

HOW WAS THE FOOD?

BREAKFAST: DELICIOUS / DECENT / DISGUSTING / DIDN'T EAT

LUNCH: DELICIOUS / DECENT / DISGUSTING / DIDN'T EAT

SNACKS: DELICIOUS / DECENT / DISGUSTING / DIDN'T EAT

QUIET   ANNOYED   COOL   SAD   TIRED   EXCITED   HAPPY   EMBARRASSED   SCARED

BORED   SICK   FRUSTRATED   ANGRY   FUNNY   PROUD   NERVOUS   GOOFY   SURPRISED

B = BEST PART OF YOUR DAY   **W** = WORST PART OF YOUR DAY   **M** = MOST OF THE DAY

RECORD IT
WHAT DID YOU LEARN TODAY?

1) ABILITY	2) SKILL	3) VOCATION	4) RELATIONSHIP	5) MENTALITY
6) MENTAL EXERCISE	7) MUSCLE MEMORY	8) PRACTICE	9) TRAINING	10) EXPERIENCE

IN THIS CLASS	I ENGAGED MOST BY ...	MINIMUM FUNCTIONALITY	THIS CLASS	MAXIMUM POSSIBILITY
	THINKING SEEING LISTENING DOING			
	THINKING SEEING LISTENING DOING			
	THINKING SEEING LISTENING DOING			
	THINKING SEEING LISTENING DOING			
	THINKING SEEING LISTENING DOING			
	THINKING SEEING LISTENING DOING			
	THINKING SEEING LISTENING DOING			
	THINKING SEEING LISTENING DOING			

THIS INSTRUCTOR	BROUGHT ME THE MOST...
	EDUCATION
	TEACHING
	FUN
	CHALLENGES

THIS...	BROUGHT ME THE MOST ISSUES
CLASS	
CONCEPT	
LESSON	
INSTRUCTOR	

THIS CLASS	WAS THE MOST...
	EDUCATIONAL
	WORK
	FUN
	BORING

MAXIMUM POSSIBILITY

1) MOTIVATION	2) INSPIRATION	3) HIGHER EDUCATION	4) CAREER	5) DREAM
6) INVENTION	7) INNOVATION	8) NON-PROFIT	9) FORTUNE 500	10) SUPERHERO

RECORD IT
HOW WAS SCHOOL TODAY?

DATE:_____

HOW DID YOU GET ALONG WITH PEOPLE?

ALLIES: POSITIVE / NEGATIVE / NEUTRAL

ANNOYANCES: POSITIVE / NEGATIVE / NEUTRAL   INSTRUCTORS: POSITIVE / NEGATIVE / NEUTRAL

HOW DID YOU BEHAVE?

SUCCESSES: MAJOR / MINOR / NONE

STRUGGLES: MAJOR / MINOR / NONE

CONFESSIONS: MAJOR / MINOR / NONE

HOW WAS YOUR ENERGY?

MORNING: FULL TANK / HALF TANK / EMPTY   NOON: FULL TANK / HALF TANK / EMPTY

AFTERNOON: FULL TANK / HALF TANK / EMPTY

DID YOU NEED THE NURSE?

HEALTH: YES / NO   INJURY: YES / NO   PAIN: YES / NO

HOW WAS THE FOOD?

BREAKFAST: DELICIOUS / DECENT / DISGUSTING / DIDN'T EAT

LUNCH: DELICIOUS / DECENT / DISGUSTING / DIDN'T EAT

SNACKS: DELICIOUS / DECENT / DISGUSTING / DIDN'T EAT

QUIET   ANNOYED   COOL   SAD   TIRED   EXCITED   HAPPY   EMBARRASSED   SCARED

BORED   SICK   FRUSTRATED   ANGRY   FUNNY   PROUD   NERVOUS   GOOFY   SURPRISED

 = BEST PART OF YOUR DAY   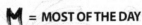 = WORST PART OF YOUR DAY   M = MOST OF THE DAY

RECORD IT
WHAT DID YOU LEARN TODAY?

MINIMUM FUNCTIONALITY

1) ABILITY	2) SKILL	3) VOCATION	4) RELATIONSHIP	5) MENTALITY
6) MENTAL EXERCISE	7) MUSCLE MEMORY	8) PRACTICE	9) TRAINING	10) EXPERIENCE

IN THIS CLASS	I ENGAGED MOST BY ...	MINIMUM FUNCTIONALITY	THIS CLASS	MAXIMUM POSSIBILITY
	THINKING SEEING LISTENING DOING			
	THINKING SEEING LISTENING DOING			
	THINKING SEEING LISTENING DOING			
	THINKING SEEING LISTENING DOING			
	THINKING SEEING LISTENING DOING			
	THINKING SEEING LISTENING DOING			
	THINKING SEEING LISTENING DOING			
	THINKING SEEING LISTENING DOING			

THIS INSTRUCTOR	BROUGHT ME THE MOST...
	EDUCATION
	TEACHING
	FUN
	CHALLENGES

THIS...	BROUGHT ME THE MOST ISSUES
CLASS	
CONCEPT	
LESSON	
INSTRUCTOR	

THIS CLASS	WAS THE MOST...
	EDUCATIONAL
	WORK
	FUN
	BORING

MAXIMUM POSSIBILITY

1) MOTIVATION	2) INSPIRATION	3) HIGHER EDUCATION	4) CAREER	5) DREAM
6) INVENTION	7) INNOVATION	8) NON-PROFIT	9) FORTUNE 500	10) SUPERHERO

RECORD IT

HOW WAS SCHOOL TODAY?

DATE:_____

HOW DID YOU GET ALONG WITH PEOPLE?

ALLIES: POSITIVE / NEGATIVE / NEUTRAL

ANNOYANCES: POSITIVE / NEGATIVE / NEUTRAL   INSTRUCTORS: POSITIVE / NEGATIVE / NEUTRAL

HOW DID YOU BEHAVE?

SUCCESSES: MAJOR / MINOR / NONE

STRUGGLES: MAJOR / MINOR / NONE

CONFESSIONS: MAJOR / MINOR / NONE

HOW WAS YOUR ENERGY?

MORNING: FULL TANK / HALF TANK / EMPTY   NOON: FULL TANK / HALF TANK / EMPTY

AFTERNOON: FULL TANK / HALF TANK / EMPTY

DID YOU NEED THE NURSE?

HEALTH: YES / NO   INJURY: YES / NO   PAIN: YES / NO

HOW WAS THE FOOD?

BREAKFAST: DELICIOUS / DECENT / DISGUSTING / DIDN'T EAT

LUNCH: DELICIOUS / DECENT / DISGUSTING / DIDN'T EAT

SNACKS: DELICIOUS / DECENT / DISGUSTING / DIDN'T EAT

 QUIET
 ANNOYED
 COOL
 SAD
 TIRED
 EXCITED
 HAPPY
 EMBARRASSED
 SCARED

 BORED
 SICK
 FRUSTRATED
 ANGRY
 FUNNY
 PROUD
NERVOUS
GOOFY
 SURPRISED

B = BEST PART OF YOUR DAY   **W** = WORST PART OF YOUR DAY   **M** = MOST OF THE DAY

RECORD IT
WHAT DID YOU LEARN TODAY?

MINIMUM FUNCTIONALITY

1) ABILITY	2) SKILL	3) VOCATION	4) RELATIONSHIP	5) MENTALITY
6) MENTAL EXERCISE	7) MUSCLE MEMORY	8) PRACTICE	9) TRAINING	10) EXPERIENCE

IN THIS CLASS	I ENGAGED MOST BY ...	MINIMUM FUNCTIONALITY	THIS CLASS	MAXIMUM POSSIBILITY
	THINKING SEEING LISTENING DOING			
	THINKING SEEING LISTENING DOING			
	THINKING SEEING LISTENING DOING			
	THINKING SEEING LISTENING DOING			
	THINKING SEEING LISTENING DOING			
	THINKING SEEING LISTENING DOING			
	THINKING SEEING LISTENING DOING			
	THINKING SEEING LISTENING DOING			

THIS INSTRUCTOR	BROUGHT ME THE MOST...
	EDUCATION
	TEACHING
	FUN
	CHALLENGES

THIS...	BROUGHT ME THE MOST ISSUES
CLASS	
CONCEPT	
LESSON	
INSTRUCTOR	

THIS CLASS	WAS THE MOST...
	EDUCATIONAL
	WORK
	FUN
	BORING

MAXIMUM POSSIBILITY

1) MOTIVATION	2) INSPIRATION	3) HIGHER EDUCATION	4) CAREER	5) DREAM
6) INVENTION	7) INNOVATION	8) NON-PROFIT	9) FORTUNE 500	10) SUPERHERO

RECORD IT
HOW WAS SCHOOL TODAY?

DATE:_____

HOW DID YOU GET ALONG WITH PEOPLE?

ALLIES: POSITIVE / NEGATIVE / NEUTRAL

ANNOYANCES: POSITIVE / NEGATIVE / NEUTRAL   INSTRUCTORS: POSITIVE / NEGATIVE / NEUTRAL

HOW DID YOU BEHAVE?

SUCCESSES: MAJOR / MINOR / NONE

STRUGGLES: MAJOR / MINOR / NONE

CONFESSIONS: MAJOR / MINOR / NONE

HOW WAS YOUR ENERGY?

MORNING: FULL TANK / HALF TANK / EMPTY   NOON: FULL TANK / HALF TANK / EMPTY

AFTERNOON: FULL TANK / HALF TANK / EMPTY

DID YOU NEED THE NURSE?

HEALTH: YES / NO   INJURY: YES / NO   PAIN: YES / NO

HOW WAS THE FOOD?

BREAKFAST: DELICIOUS / DECENT / DISGUSTING / DIDN'T EAT

LUNCH: DELICIOUS / DECENT / DISGUSTING / DIDN'T EAT

SNACKS: DELICIOUS / DECENT / DISGUSTING / DIDN'T EAT

QUIET   ANNOYED   COOL   SAD   TIRED   EXCITED   HAPPY   EMBARRASSED   SCARED

BORED   SICK   FRUSTRATED   ANGRY   FUNNY   PROUD   NERVOUS   GOOFY   SURPRISED

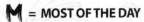

B = BEST PART OF YOUR DAY   W = WORST PART OF YOUR DAY   M = MOST OF THE DAY

RECORD IT
WHAT DID YOU LEARN TODAY?

1) ABILITY	2) SKILL	3) VOCATION	4) RELATIONSHIP	5) MENTALITY
6) MENTAL EXERCISE	7) MUSCLE MEMORY	8) PRACTICE	9) TRAINING	10) EXPERIENCE

IN THIS CLASS	I ENGAGED MOST BY ...	MINIMUM FUNCTIONALITY	THIS CLASS	MAXIMUM POSSIBILITY
	THINKING SEEING LISTENING DOING			
	THINKING SEEING LISTENING DOING			
	THINKING SEEING LISTENING DOING			
	THINKING SEEING LISTENING DOING			
	THINKING SEEING LISTENING DOING			
	THINKING SEEING LISTENING DOING			
	THINKING SEEING LISTENING DOING			
	THINKING SEEING LISTENING DOING			

THIS INSTRUCTOR	BROUGHT ME THE MOST...
	EDUCATION
	TEACHING
	FUN
	CHALLENGES

THIS...	BROUGHT ME THE MOST ISSUES
CLASS	
CONCEPT	
LESSON	
INSTRUCTOR	

THIS CLASS	WAS THE MOST...
	EDUCATIONAL
	WORK
	FUN
	BORING

MAXIMUM POSSIBILITY

1) MOTIVATION	2) INSPIRATION	3) HIGHER EDUCATION	4) CAREER	5) DREAM
6) INVENTION	7) INNOVATION	8) NON-PROFIT	9) FORTUNE 500	10) SUPERHERO

RECORD IT
HOW WAS SCHOOL TODAY?

DATE:_____

HOW DID YOU GET ALONG WITH PEOPLE?

ALLIES: POSITIVE / NEGATIVE / NEUTRAL

ANNOYANCES: POSITIVE / NEGATIVE / NEUTRAL   INSTRUCTORS: POSITIVE / NEGATIVE / NEUTRAL

HOW DID YOU BEHAVE?

SUCCESSES: MAJOR / MINOR / NONE

STRUGGLES: MAJOR / MINOR / NONE

CONFESSIONS: MAJOR / MINOR / NONE

HOW WAS YOUR ENERGY?

MORNING: FULL TANK / HALF TANK / EMPTY   NOON: FULL TANK / HALF TANK / EMPTY

AFTERNOON: FULL TANK / HALF TANK / EMPTY

DID YOU NEED THE NURSE?

HEALTH: YES / NO   INJURY: YES / NO   PAIN: YES / NO

HOW WAS THE FOOD?

BREAKFAST: DELICIOUS / DECENT / DISGUSTING / DIDN'T EAT

LUNCH: DELICIOUS / DECENT / DISGUSTING / DIDN'T EAT

SNACKS: DELICIOUS / DECENT / DISGUSTING / DIDN'T EAT

QUIET   ANNOYED   COOL   SAD   TIRED   EXCITED   HAPPY   EMBARRASSED   SCARED

BORED   SICK   FRUSTRATED   ANGRY   FUNNY   PROUD   NERVOUS   GOOFY   SURPRISED

B = BEST PART OF YOUR DAY   **W** = WORST PART OF YOUR DAY   **M** = MOST OF THE DAY

RECORD IT
WHAT DID YOU LEARN TODAY?

MINIMUM FUNCTIONALITY

1) ABILITY	2) SKILL	3) VOCATION	4) RELATIONSHIP	5) MENTALITY
6) MENTAL EXERCISE	7) MUSCLE MEMORY	8) PRACTICE	9) TRAINING	10) EXPERIENCE

IN THIS CLASS	I ENGAGED MOST BY …	MINIMUM FUNCTIONALITY	THIS CLASS	MAXIMUM POSSIBILITY
	THINKING SEEING LISTENING DOING			
	THINKING SEEING LISTENING DOING			
	THINKING SEEING LISTENING DOING			
	THINKING SEEING LISTENING DOING			
	THINKING SEEING LISTENING DOING			
	THINKING SEEING LISTENING DOING			
	THINKING SEEING LISTENING DOING			
	THINKING SEEING LISTENING DOING			

THIS INSTRUCTOR	BROUGHT ME THE MOST…
	EDUCATION
	TEACHING
	FUN
	CHALLENGES

THIS…	BROUGHT ME THE MOST ISSUES
CLASS	
CONCEPT	
LESSON	
INSTRUCTOR	

THIS CLASS	WAS THE MOST…
	EDUCATIONAL
	WORK
	FUN
	BORING

MAXIMUM POSSIBILITY

1) MOTIVATION	2) INSPIRATION	3) HIGHER EDUCATION	4) CAREER	5) DREAM
6) INVENTION	7) INNOVATION	8) NON-PROFIT	9) FORTUNE 500	10) SUPERHERO

HOW WAS SCHOOL TODAY?

DATE:_____

HOW DID YOU GET ALONG WITH PEOPLE?

ALLIES: POSITIVE / NEGATIVE / NEUTRAL

ANNOYANCES: POSITIVE / NEGATIVE / NEUTRAL   INSTRUCTORS: POSITIVE / NEGATIVE / NEUTRAL

HOW DID YOU BEHAVE?

SUCCESSES: MAJOR / MINOR / NONE

STRUGGLES: MAJOR / MINOR / NONE

CONFESSIONS: MAJOR / MINOR / NONE

HOW WAS YOUR ENERGY?

MORNING: FULL TANK / HALF TANK / EMPTY   NOON: FULL TANK / HALF TANK / EMPTY

AFTERNOON: FULL TANK / HALF TANK / EMPTY

DID YOU NEED THE NURSE?

HEALTH: YES / NO   INJURY: YES / NO   PAIN: YES / NO

HOW WAS THE FOOD?

BREAKFAST: DELICIOUS / DECENT / DISGUSTING / DIDN'T EAT

LUNCH: DELICIOUS / DECENT / DISGUSTING / DIDN'T EAT

SNACKS: DELICIOUS / DECENT / DISGUSTING / DIDN'T EAT

QUIET   ANNOYED   COOL   SAD   TIRED   EXCITED   HAPPY   EMBARRASSED   SCARED

BORED   SICK   FRUSTRATED   ANGRY   FUNNY   PROUD   NERVOUS   GOOFY   SURPRISED

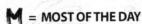

B = BEST PART OF YOUR DAY   **W** = WORST PART OF YOUR DAY   **M** = MOST OF THE DAY

RECORD IT
WHAT DID YOU LEARN TODAY?

MINIMUM FUNCTIONALITY

1) ABILITY	2) SKILL	3) VOCATION	4) RELATIONSHIP	5) MENTALITY
6) MENTAL EXERCISE	7) MUSCLE MEMORY	8) PRACTICE	9) TRAINING	10) EXPERIENCE

IN THIS CLASS	I ENGAGED MOST BY ...		MINIMUM FUNCTIONALITY	THIS CLASS	MAXIMUM POSSIBILITY
	THINKING SEEING LISTENING DOING				
	THINKING SEEING LISTENING DOING				
	THINKING SEEING LISTENING DOING				
	THINKING SEEING LISTENING DOING				
	THINKING SEEING LISTENING DOING				
	THINKING SEEING LISTENING DOING				
	THINKING SEEING LISTENING DOING				
	THINKING SEEING LISTENING DOING				

THIS INSTRUCTOR	BROUGHT ME THE MOST...
	EDUCATION
	TEACHING
	FUN
	CHALLENGES

THIS...	BROUGHT ME THE MOST ISSUES
CLASS	
CONCEPT	
LESSON	
INSTRUCTOR	

THIS CLASS	WAS THE MOST...
	EDUCATIONAL
	WORK
	FUN
	BORING

MAXIMUM POSSIBILITY

1) MOTIVATION	2) INSPIRATION	3) HIGHER EDUCATION	4) CAREER	5) DREAM
6) INVENTION	7) INNOVATION	8) NON-PROFIT	9) FORTUNE 500	10) SUPERHERO

RECORD IT
HOW WAS SCHOOL TODAY?

DATE:_____

HOW DID YOU GET ALONG WITH PEOPLE?

ALLIES: POSITIVE / NEGATIVE / NEUTRAL

ANNOYANCES: POSITIVE / NEGATIVE / NEUTRAL   INSTRUCTORS: POSITIVE / NEGATIVE / NEUTRAL

HOW DID YOU BEHAVE?

SUCCESSES: MAJOR / MINOR / NONE

STRUGGLES: MAJOR / MINOR / NONE

CONFESSIONS: MAJOR / MINOR / NONE

HOW WAS YOUR ENERGY?

MORNING: FULL TANK / HALF TANK / EMPTY   NOON: FULL TANK / HALF TANK / EMPTY

AFTERNOON: FULL TANK / HALF TANK / EMPTY

DID YOU NEED THE NURSE?

HEALTH: YES / NO   INJURY: YES / NO   PAIN: YES / NO

HOW WAS THE FOOD?

BREAKFAST: DELICIOUS / DECENT / DISGUSTING / DIDN'T EAT

LUNCH: DELICIOUS / DECENT / DISGUSTING / DIDN'T EAT

SNACKS: DELICIOUS / DECENT / DISGUSTING / DIDN'T EAT

QUIET   ANNOYED   COOL   SAD   TIRED   EXCITED   HAPPY   EMBARRASSED   SCARED

BORED   SICK   FRUSTRATED   ANGRY   FUNNY   PROUD   NERVOUS   GOOFY   SURPRISED

B = BEST PART OF YOUR DAY   **W** = WORST PART OF YOUR DAY   **M** = MOST OF THE DAY

RECORD IT
WHAT DID YOU LEARN TODAY?

MINIMUM FUNCTIONALITY

1) ABILITY	2) SKILL	3) VOCATION	4) RELATIONSHIP	5) MENTALITY
6) MENTAL EXERCISE	7) MUSCLE MEMORY	8) PRACTICE	9) TRAINING	10) EXPERIENCE

IN THIS CLASS	I ENGAGED MOST BY ...	MINIMUM FUNCTIONALITY	THIS CLASS	MAXIMUM POSSIBILITY
	THINKING SEEING LISTENING DOING			
	THINKING SEEING LISTENING DOING			
	THINKING SEEING LISTENING DOING			
	THINKING SEEING LISTENING DOING			
	THINKING SEEING LISTENING DOING			
	THINKING SEEING LISTENING DOING			
	THINKING SEEING LISTENING DOING			
	THINKING SEEING LISTENING DOING			

THIS INSTRUCTOR	BROUGHT ME THE MOST...
	EDUCATION
	TEACHING
	FUN
	CHALLENGES

THIS...	BROUGHT ME THE MOST ISSUES
CLASS	
CONCEPT	
LESSON	
INSTRUCTOR	

THIS CLASS	WAS THE MOST...
	EDUCATIONAL
	WORK
	FUN
	BORING

MAXIMUM POSSIBILITY

1) MOTIVATION	2) INSPIRATION	3) HIGHER EDUCATION	4) CAREER	5) DREAM
6) INVENTION	7) INNOVATION	8) NON-PROFIT	9) FORTUNE 500	10) SUPERHERO

RECORD IT
HOW WAS SCHOOL TODAY?

DATE:_____

HOW DID YOU GET ALONG WITH PEOPLE?

ALLIES: POSITIVE / NEGATIVE / NEUTRAL

ANNOYANCES: POSITIVE / NEGATIVE / NEUTRAL   INSTRUCTORS: POSITIVE / NEGATIVE / NEUTRAL

HOW DID YOU BEHAVE?

SUCCESSES: MAJOR / MINOR / NONE

STRUGGLES: MAJOR / MINOR / NONE

CONFESSIONS: MAJOR / MINOR / NONE

HOW WAS YOUR ENERGY?

MORNING: FULL TANK / HALF TANK / EMPTY   NOON: FULL TANK / HALF TANK / EMPTY

AFTERNOON: FULL TANK / HALF TANK / EMPTY

DID YOU NEED THE NURSE?

HEALTH: YES / NO   INJURY: YES / NO   PAIN: YES / NO

HOW WAS THE FOOD?

BREAKFAST: DELICIOUS / DECENT / DISGUSTING / DIDN'T EAT

LUNCH: DELICIOUS / DECENT / DISGUSTING / DIDN'T EAT

SNACKS: DELICIOUS / DECENT / DISGUSTING / DIDN'T EAT

QUIET   ANNOYED   COOL   SAD   TIRED   EXCITED   HAPPY   EMBARRASSED   SCARED

BORED   SICK   FRUSTRATED   ANGRY   FUNNY   PROUD   NERVOUS   GOOFY   SURPRISED

B = BEST PART OF YOUR DAY   **W** = WORST PART OF YOUR DAY   **M** = MOST OF THE DAY

RECORD IT
WHAT DID YOU LEARN TODAY?

MINIMUM FUNCTIONALITY

1) ABILITY	2) SKILL	3) VOCATION	4) RELATIONSHIP	5) MENTALITY
6) MENTAL EXERCISE	7) MUSCLE MEMORY	8) PRACTICE	9) TRAINING	10) EXPERIENCE

IN THIS CLASS	I ENGAGED MOST BY ...	MINIMUM FUNCTIONALITY	THIS CLASS	MAXIMUM POSSIBILITY
	THINKING SEEING LISTENING DOING			
	THINKING SEEING LISTENING DOING			
	THINKING SEEING LISTENING DOING			
	THINKING SEEING LISTENING DOING			
	THINKING SEEING LISTENING DOING			
	THINKING SEEING LISTENING DOING			
	THINKING SEEING LISTENING DOING			
	THINKING SEEING LISTENING DOING			

THIS INSTRUCTOR	BROUGHT ME THE MOST...
	EDUCATION
	TEACHING
	FUN
	CHALLENGES

THIS...	BROUGHT ME THE MOST ISSUES
CLASS	
CONCEPT	
LESSON	
INSTRUCTOR	

THIS CLASS	WAS THE MOST...
	EDUCATIONAL
	WORK
	FUN
	BORING

MAXIMUM POSSIBILITY

1) MOTIVATION	2) INSPIRATION	3) HIGHER EDUCATION	4) CAREER	5) DREAM
6) INVENTION	7) INNOVATION	8) NON-PROFIT	9) FORTUNE 500	10) SUPERHERO

RECORD IT
HOW WAS SCHOOL TODAY?

DATE:_____

HOW DID YOU GET ALONG WITH PEOPLE?

ALLIES: POSITIVE / NEGATIVE / NEUTRAL

ANNOYANCES: POSITIVE / NEGATIVE / NEUTRAL   INSTRUCTORS: POSITIVE / NEGATIVE / NEUTRAL

HOW DID YOU BEHAVE?

SUCCESSES: MAJOR / MINOR / NONE

STRUGGLES: MAJOR / MINOR / NONE

CONFESSIONS: MAJOR / MINOR / NONE

HOW WAS YOUR ENERGY?

MORNING: FULL TANK / HALF TANK / EMPTY   NOON: FULL TANK / HALF TANK / EMPTY

AFTERNOON: FULL TANK / HALF TANK / EMPTY

DID YOU NEED THE NURSE?

HEALTH: YES / NO   INJURY: YES / NO   PAIN: YES / NO

HOW WAS THE FOOD?

BREAKFAST: DELICIOUS / DECENT / DISGUSTING / DIDN'T EAT

LUNCH: DELICIOUS / DECENT / DISGUSTING / DIDN'T EAT

SNACKS: DELICIOUS / DECENT / DISGUSTING / DIDN'T EAT

QUIET   ANNOYED   COOL   SAD   TIRED   EXCITED   HAPPY   EMBARRASSED   SCARED

BORED   SICK   FRUSTRATED   ANGRY   FUNNY   PROUD   NERVOUS   GOOFY   SURPRISED

B = BEST PART OF YOUR DAY   **W** = WORST PART OF YOUR DAY   **M** = MOST OF THE DAY

RECORD IT
WHAT DID YOU LEARN TODAY?

MINIMUM FUNCTIONALITY

1) ABILITY	2) SKILL	3) VOCATION	4) RELATIONSHIP	5) MENTALITY
6) MENTAL EXERCISE	7) MUSCLE MEMORY	8) PRACTICE	9) TRAINING	10) EXPERIENCE

IN THIS CLASS	I ENGAGED MOST BY ...	MINIMUM FUNCTIONALITY	THIS CLASS	MAXIMUM POSSIBILITY
	THINKING SEEING LISTENING DOING			
	THINKING SEEING LISTENING DOING			
	THINKING SEEING LISTENING DOING			
	THINKING SEEING LISTENING DOING			
	THINKING SEEING LISTENING DOING			
	THINKING SEEING LISTENING DOING			
	THINKING SEEING LISTENING DOING			
	THINKING SEEING LISTENING DOING			

THIS INSTRUCTOR	BROUGHT ME THE MOST...
	EDUCATION
	TEACHING
	FUN
	CHALLENGES

THIS...	BROUGHT ME THE MOST ISSUES
CLASS	
CONCEPT	
LESSON	
INSTRUCTOR	

THIS CLASS	WAS THE MOST...
	EDUCATIONAL
	WORK
	FUN
	BORING

MAXIMUM POSSIBILITY

1) MOTIVATION	2) INSPIRATION	3) HIGHER EDUCATION	4) CAREER	5) DREAM
6) INVENTION	7) INNOVATION	8) NON-PROFIT	9) FORTUNE 500	10) SUPERHERO

RECORD IT
HOW WAS SCHOOL TODAY?

DATE:_____

HOW DID YOU GET ALONG WITH PEOPLE?

ALLIES: POSITIVE / NEGATIVE / NEUTRAL

ANNOYANCES: POSITIVE / NEGATIVE / NEUTRAL   INSTRUCTORS: POSITIVE / NEGATIVE / NEUTRAL

HOW DID YOU BEHAVE?

SUCCESSES: MAJOR / MINOR / NONE

STRUGGLES: MAJOR / MINOR / NONE

CONFESSIONS: MAJOR / MINOR / NONE

HOW WAS YOUR ENERGY?

MORNING: FULL TANK / HALF TANK / EMPTY   NOON: FULL TANK / HALF TANK / EMPTY

AFTERNOON: FULL TANK / HALF TANK / EMPTY

DID YOU NEED THE NURSE?

HEALTH: YES / NO   INJURY: YES / NO   PAIN: YES / NO

HOW WAS THE FOOD?

BREAKFAST: DELICIOUS / DECENT / DISGUSTING / DIDN'T EAT

LUNCH: DELICIOUS / DECENT / DISGUSTING / DIDN'T EAT

SNACKS: DELICIOUS / DECENT / DISGUSTING / DIDN'T EAT

QUIET   ANNOYED   COOL   SAD   TIRED   EXCITED   HAPPY   EMBARRASSED   SCARED

BORED   SICK   FRUSTRATED   ANGRY   FUNNY   PROUD   NERVOUS   GOOFY   SURPRISED

B = BEST PART OF YOUR DAY   **W** = WORST PART OF YOUR DAY   **M** = MOST OF THE DAY

RECORD IT
WHAT DID YOU LEARN TODAY?

MINIMUM FUNCTIONALITY

1) ABILITY	2) SKILL	3) VOCATION	4) RELATIONSHIP	5) MENTALITY
6) MENTAL EXERCISE	7) MUSCLE MEMORY	8) PRACTICE	9) TRAINING	10) EXPERIENCE

IN THIS CLASS	I ENGAGED MOST BY ...	MINIMUM FUNCTIONALITY	THIS CLASS	MAXIMUM POSSIBILITY
	THINKING SEEING LISTENING DOING			
	THINKING SEEING LISTENING DOING			
	THINKING SEEING LISTENING DOING			
	THINKING SEEING LISTENING DOING			
	THINKING SEEING LISTENING DOING			
	THINKING SEEING LISTENING DOING			
	THINKING SEEING LISTENING DOING			
	THINKING SEEING LISTENING DOING			

THIS INSTRUCTOR	BROUGHT ME THE MOST...
	EDUCATION
	TEACHING
	FUN
	CHALLENGES

THIS...	BROUGHT ME THE MOST ISSUES
CLASS	
CONCEPT	
LESSON	
INSTRUCTOR	

THIS CLASS	WAS THE MOST...
	EDUCATIONAL
	WORK
	FUN
	BORING

MAXIMUM POSSIBILITY

1) MOTIVATION	2) INSPIRATION	3) HIGHER EDUCATION	4) CAREER	5) DREAM
6) INVENTION	7) INNOVATION	8) NON-PROFIT	9) FORTUNE 500	10) SUPERHERO

How Was School Today?

DATE:_____

HOW DID YOU GET ALONG WITH PEOPLE?

ALLIES: POSITIVE / NEGATIVE / NEUTRAL

ANNOYANCES: POSITIVE / NEGATIVE / NEUTRAL   INSTRUCTORS: POSITIVE / NEGATIVE / NEUTRAL

HOW DID YOU BEHAVE?

SUCCESSES: MAJOR / MINOR / NONE

STRUGGLES: MAJOR / MINOR / NONE

CONFESSIONS: MAJOR / MINOR / NONE

HOW WAS YOUR ENERGY?

MORNING: FULL TANK / HALF TANK / EMPTY   NOON: FULL TANK / HALF TANK / EMPTY

AFTERNOON: FULL TANK / HALF TANK / EMPTY

DID YOU NEED THE NURSE?

HEALTH: YES / NO   INJURY: YES / NO   PAIN: YES / NO

HOW WAS THE FOOD?

BREAKFAST: DELICIOUS / DECENT / DISGUSTING / DIDN'T EAT

LUNCH: DELICIOUS / DECENT / DISGUSTING / DIDN'T EAT

SNACKS: DELICIOUS / DECENT / DISGUSTING / DIDN'T EAT

QUIET   ANNOYED   COOL   SAD   TIRED   EXCITED   HAPPY   EMBARRASSED   SCARED

         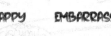

BORED   SICK   FRUSTRATED   ANGRY   FUNNY   PROUD   NERVOUS   GOOFY   SURPRISED

B = BEST PART OF YOUR DAY   **W** = WORST PART OF YOUR DAY   **M** = MOST OF THE DAY

RECORD IT
WHAT DID YOU LEARN TODAY?

MINIMUM FUNCTIONALITY

1) ABILITY	2) SKILL	3) VOCATION	4) RELATIONSHIP	5) MENTALITY
6) MENTAL EXERCISE	7) MUSCLE MEMORY	8) PRACTICE	9) TRAINING	10) EXPERIENCE

IN THIS CLASS	I ENGAGED MOST BY ...	MINIMUM FUNCTIONALITY	THIS CLASS	MAXIMUM POSSIBILITY
	THINKING SEEING LISTENING DOING			
	THINKING SEEING LISTENING DOING			
	THINKING SEEING LISTENING DOING			
	THINKING SEEING LISTENING DOING			
	THINKING SEEING LISTENING DOING			
	THINKING SEEING LISTENING DOING			
	THINKING SEEING LISTENING DOING			
	THINKING SEEING LISTENING DOING			

THIS INSTRUCTOR	BROUGHT ME THE MOST...
	EDUCATION
	TEACHING
	FUN
	CHALLENGES

THIS...	BROUGHT ME THE MOST ISSUES
CLASS	
CONCEPT	
LESSON	
INSTRUCTOR	

THIS CLASS	WAS THE MOST...
	EDUCATIONAL
	WORK
	FUN
	BORING

MAXIMUM POSSIBILITY

1) MOTIVATION	2) INSPIRATION	3) HIGHER EDUCATION	4) CAREER	5) DREAM
6) INVENTION	7) INNOVATION	8) NON-PROFIT	9) FORTUNE 500	10) SUPERHERO

RECORD IT
HOW WAS SCHOOL TODAY?

DATE:_____

HOW DID YOU GET ALONG WITH PEOPLE?

ALLIES: POSITIVE / NEGATIVE / NEUTRAL

ANNOYANCES: POSITIVE / NEGATIVE / NEUTRAL   INSTRUCTORS: POSITIVE / NEGATIVE / NEUTRAL

HOW DID YOU BEHAVE?

SUCCESSES: MAJOR / MINOR / NONE

STRUGGLES: MAJOR / MINOR / NONE

CONFESSIONS: MAJOR / MINOR / NONE

HOW WAS YOUR ENERGY?

MORNING: FULL TANK / HALF TANK / EMPTY   NOON: FULL TANK / HALF TANK / EMPTY

AFTERNOON: FULL TANK / HALF TANK / EMPTY

DID YOU NEED THE NURSE?

HEALTH: YES / NO   INJURY: YES / NO   PAIN: YES / NO

HOW WAS THE FOOD?

BREAKFAST: DELICIOUS / DECENT / DISGUSTING / DIDN'T EAT

LUNCH: DELICIOUS / DECENT / DISGUSTING / DIDN'T EAT

SNACKS: DELICIOUS / DECENT / DISGUSTING / DIDN'T EAT

QUIET   ANNOYED   COOL   SAD   TIRED   EXCITED   HAPPY   EMBARRASSED   SCARED

BORED   SICK   FRUSTRATED   ANGRY   FUNNY   PROUD   NERVOUS   GOOFY   SURPRISED

B = BEST PART OF YOUR DAY   **W** = WORST PART OF YOUR DAY   **M** = MOST OF THE DAY

RECORD IT
WHAT DID YOU LEARN TODAY?

1) ABILITY	2) SKILL	3) VOCATION	4) RELATIONSHIP	5) MENTALITY
6) MENTAL EXERCISE	7) MUSCLE MEMORY	8) PRACTICE	9) TRAINING	10) EXPERIENCE

IN THIS CLASS	I ENGAGED MOST BY ...	MINIMUM FUNCTIONALITY	THIS CLASS	MAXIMUM POSSIBILITY
	THINKING SEEING LISTENING DOING			
	THINKING SEEING LISTENING DOING			
	THINKING SEEING LISTENING DOING			
	THINKING SEEING LISTENING DOING			
	THINKING SEEING LISTENING DOING			
	THINKING SEEING LISTENING DOING			
	THINKING SEEING LISTENING DOING			
	THINKING SEEING LISTENING DOING			

THIS INSTRUCTOR	BROUGHT ME THE MOST...
	EDUCATION
	TEACHING
	FUN
	CHALLENGES

THIS...	BROUGHT ME THE MOST ISSUES
CLASS	
CONCEPT	
LESSON	
INSTRUCTOR	

THIS CLASS	WAS THE MOST...
	EDUCATIONAL
	WORK
	FUN
	BORING

MAXIMUM POSSIBILITY

1) MOTIVATION	2) INSPIRATION	3) HIGHER EDUCATION	4) CAREER	5) DREAM
6) INVENTION	7) INNOVATION	8) NON-PROFIT	9) FORTUNE 500	10) SUPERHERO

RECORD IT

How Was School Today?

DATE:_____

HOW DID YOU GET ALONG WITH PEOPLE?

ALLIES: POSITIVE / NEGATIVE / NEUTRAL

ANNOYANCES: POSITIVE / NEGATIVE / NEUTRAL   INSTRUCTORS: POSITIVE / NEGATIVE / NEUTRAL

HOW DID YOU BEHAVE?

SUCCESSES: MAJOR / MINOR / NONE

STRUGGLES: MAJOR / MINOR / NONE

CONFESSIONS: MAJOR / MINOR / NONE

HOW WAS YOUR ENERGY?

MORNING: FULL TANK / HALF TANK / EMPTY   NOON: FULL TANK / HALF TANK / EMPTY

AFTERNOON: FULL TANK / HALF TANK / EMPTY

DID YOU NEED THE NURSE?

HEALTH: YES / NO   INJURY: YES / NO   PAIN: YES / NO

HOW WAS THE FOOD?

BREAKFAST: DELICIOUS / DECENT / DISGUSTING / DIDN'T EAT

LUNCH: DELICIOUS / DECENT / DISGUSTING / DIDN'T EAT

SNACKS: DELICIOUS / DECENT / DISGUSTING / DIDN'T EAT

 QUIET ANNOYED COOL SAD TIRED EXCITED HAPPY EMBARRASSED SCARED

 BORED SICK FRUSTRATED ANGRY FUNNY PROUD NERVOUS GOOFY SURPRISED

B = BEST PART OF YOUR DAY   W = WORST PART OF YOUR DAY   M = MOST OF THE DAY

RECORD IT
WHAT DID YOU LEARN TODAY?

MINIMUM FUNCTIONALITY

1) ABILITY	2) SKILL	3) VOCATION	4) RELATIONSHIP	5) MENTALITY
6) MENTAL EXERCISE	7) MUSCLE MEMORY	8) PRACTICE	9) TRAINING	10) EXPERIENCE

IN THIS CLASS	I ENGAGED MOST BY ...	MINIMUM FUNCTIONALITY	THIS CLASS	MAXIMUM POSSIBILITY
	THINKING SEEING LISTENING DOING			
	THINKING SEEING LISTENING DOING			
	THINKING SEEING LISTENING DOING			
	THINKING SEEING LISTENING DOING			
	THINKING SEEING LISTENING DOING			
	THINKING SEEING LISTENING DOING			
	THINKING SEEING LISTENING DOING			
	THINKING SEEING LISTENING DOING			

THIS INSTRUCTOR	BROUGHT ME THE MOST...
	EDUCATION
	TEACHING
	FUN
	CHALLENGES

THIS...	BROUGHT ME THE MOST ISSUES
CLASS	
CONCEPT	
LESSON	
INSTRUCTOR	

THIS CLASS	WAS THE MOST...
	EDUCATIONAL
	WORK
	FUN
	BORING

MAXIMUM POSSIBILITY

1) MOTIVATION	2) INSPIRATION	3) HIGHER EDUCATION	4) CAREER	5) DREAM
6) INVENTION	7) INNOVATION	8) NON-PROFIT	9) FORTUNE 500	10) SUPERHERO

RECORD IT
HOW WAS SCHOOL TODAY?

DATE:_____

HOW DID YOU GET ALONG WITH PEOPLE?

ALLIES: POSITIVE / NEGATIVE / NEUTRAL

ANNOYANCES: POSITIVE / NEGATIVE / NEUTRAL   INSTRUCTORS: POSITIVE / NEGATIVE / NEUTRAL

HOW DID YOU BEHAVE?

SUCCESSES: MAJOR / MINOR / NONE

STRUGGLES: MAJOR / MINOR / NONE

CONFESSIONS: MAJOR / MINOR / NONE

HOW WAS YOUR ENERGY?

MORNING: FULL TANK / HALF TANK / EMPTY   NOON: FULL TANK / HALF TANK / EMPTY

AFTERNOON: FULL TANK / HALF TANK / EMPTY

DID YOU NEED THE NURSE?

HEALTH: YES / NO   INJURY: YES / NO   PAIN: YES / NO

HOW WAS THE FOOD?

BREAKFAST: DELICIOUS / DECENT / DISGUSTING / DIDN'T EAT

LUNCH: DELICIOUS / DECENT / DISGUSTING / DIDN'T EAT

SNACKS: DELICIOUS / DECENT / DISGUSTING / DIDN'T EAT

QUIET   ANNOYED   COOL   SAD   TIRED   EXCITED   HAPPY   EMBARRASSED   SCARED

BORED   SICK   FRUSTRATED   ANGRY   FUNNY   PROUD   NERVOUS   GOOFY   SURPRISED

B = BEST PART OF YOUR DAY   **W** = WORST PART OF YOUR DAY   **M** = MOST OF THE DAY

RECORD IT
WHAT DID YOU LEARN TODAY?

MINIMUM FUNCTIONALITY

1) ABILITY	2) SKILL	3) VOCATION	4) RELATIONSHIP	5) MENTALITY
6) MENTAL EXERCISE	7) MUSCLE MEMORY	8) PRACTICE	9) TRAINING	10) EXPERIENCE

IN THIS CLASS	I ENGAGED MOST BY ...	MINIMUM FUNCTIONALITY	THIS CLASS	MAXIMUM POSSIBILITY
	THINKING SEEING LISTENING DOING			
	THINKING SEEING LISTENING DOING			
	THINKING SEEING LISTENING DOING			
	THINKING SEEING LISTENING DOING			
	THINKING SEEING LISTENING DOING			
	THINKING SEEING LISTENING DOING			
	THINKING SEEING LISTENING DOING			
	THINKING SEEING LISTENING DOING			

THIS INSTRUCTOR	BROUGHT ME THE MOST...
	EDUCATION
	TEACHING
	FUN
	CHALLENGES

THIS...	BROUGHT ME THE MOST ISSUES
CLASS	
CONCEPT	
LESSON	
INSTRUCTOR	

THIS CLASS	WAS THE MOST...
	EDUCATIONAL
	WORK
	FUN
	BORING

MAXIMUM POSSIBILITY

1) MOTIVATION	2) INSPIRATION	3) HIGHER EDUCATION	4) CAREER	5) DREAM
6) INVENTION	7) INNOVATION	8) NON-PROFIT	9) FORTUNE 500	10) SUPERHERO

RECORD IT
How Was School Today?

DATE:_____

HOW DID YOU GET ALONG WITH PEOPLE?

ALLIES: POSITIVE / NEGATIVE / NEUTRAL

ANNOYANCES: POSITIVE / NEGATIVE / NEUTRAL   INSTRUCTORS: POSITIVE / NEGATIVE / NEUTRAL

HOW DID YOU BEHAVE?

SUCCESSES: MAJOR / MINOR / NONE

STRUGGLES: MAJOR / MINOR / NONE

CONFESSIONS: MAJOR / MINOR / NONE

HOW WAS YOUR ENERGY?

MORNING: FULL TANK / HALF TANK / EMPTY   NOON: FULL TANK / HALF TANK / EMPTY

AFTERNOON: FULL TANK / HALF TANK / EMPTY

DID YOU NEED THE NURSE?

HEALTH: YES / NO   INJURY: YES / NO   PAIN: YES / NO

HOW WAS THE FOOD?

BREAKFAST: DELICIOUS / DECENT / DISGUSTING / DIDN'T EAT

LUNCH: DELICIOUS / DECENT / DISGUSTING / DIDN'T EAT

SNACKS: DELICIOUS / DECENT / DISGUSTING / DIDN'T EAT

QUIET   ANNOYED   COOL   SAD   TIRED   EXCITED   HAPPY   EMBARRASSED   SCARED

BORED   SICK   FRUSTRATED   ANGRY   FUNNY   PROUD   NERVOUS   GOOFY   SURPRISED

B = BEST PART OF YOUR DAY   W = WORST PART OF YOUR DAY   M = MOST OF THE DAY

RECORD IT
WHAT DID YOU LEARN TODAY?

MINIMUM FUNCTIONALITY

1) ABILITY	2) SKILL	3) VOCATION	4) RELATIONSHIP	5) MENTALITY
6) MENTAL EXERCISE	7) MUSCLE MEMORY	8) PRACTICE	9) TRAINING	10) EXPERIENCE

IN THIS CLASS	I ENGAGED MOST BY ...	MINIMUM FUNCTIONALITY	THIS CLASS	MAXIMUM POSSIBILITY
	THINKING SEEING LISTENING DOING			
	THINKING SEEING LISTENING DOING			
	THINKING SEEING LISTENING DOING			
	THINKING SEEING LISTENING DOING			
	THINKING SEEING LISTENING DOING			
	THINKING SEEING LISTENING DOING			
	THINKING SEEING LISTENING DOING			
	THINKING SEEING LISTENING DOING			

THIS INSTRUCTOR	BROUGHT ME THE MOST...
	EDUCATION
	TEACHING
	FUN
	CHALLENGES

THIS...	BROUGHT ME THE MOST ISSUES
CLASS	
CONCEPT	
LESSON	
INSTRUCTOR	

THIS CLASS	WAS THE MOST...
	EDUCATIONAL
	WORK
	FUN
	BORING

MAXIMUM POSSIBILITY

1) MOTIVATION	2) INSPIRATION	3) HIGHER EDUCATION	4) CAREER	5) DREAM
6) INVENTION	7) INNOVATION	8) NON-PROFIT	9) FORTUNE 500	10) SUPERHERO

RECORD IT
HOW WAS SCHOOL TODAY?

DATE:_____

HOW DID YOU GET ALONG WITH PEOPLE?

ALLIES: POSITIVE / NEGATIVE / NEUTRAL

ANNOYANCES: POSITIVE / NEGATIVE / NEUTRAL   INSTRUCTORS: POSITIVE / NEGATIVE / NEUTRAL

HOW DID YOU BEHAVE?

SUCCESSES: MAJOR / MINOR / NONE

STRUGGLES: MAJOR / MINOR / NONE

CONFESSIONS: MAJOR / MINOR / NONE

HOW WAS YOUR ENERGY?

MORNING: FULL TANK / HALF TANK / EMPTY   NOON: FULL TANK / HALF TANK / EMPTY

AFTERNOON: FULL TANK / HALF TANK / EMPTY

DID YOU NEED THE NURSE?

HEALTH: YES / NO   INJURY: YES / NO   PAIN: YES / NO

HOW WAS THE FOOD?

BREAKFAST: DELICIOUS / DECENT / DISGUSTING / DIDN'T EAT

LUNCH: DELICIOUS / DECENT / DISGUSTING / DIDN'T EAT

SNACKS: DELICIOUS / DECENT / DISGUSTING / DIDN'T EAT

 QUIET
 ANNOYED
 COOL
 SAD
 TIRED
 EXCITED
 HAPPY
 EMBARRASSED
 SCARED

 BORED
 SICK
 FRUSTRATED
 ANGRY
 FUNNY
 PROUD
 NERVOUS
 GOOFY
SURPRISED

B = BEST PART OF YOUR DAY   **W** = WORST PART OF YOUR DAY   **M** = MOST OF THE DAY

RECORD IT
WHAT DID YOU LEARN TODAY?

MINIMUM FUNCTIONALITY

1) ABILITY	2) SKILL	3) VOCATION	4) RELATIONSHIP	5) MENTALITY
6) MENTAL EXERCISE	7) MUSCLE MEMORY	8) PRACTICE	9) TRAINING	10) EXPERIENCE

IN THIS CLASS	I ENGAGED MOST BY ...	MINIMUM FUNCTIONALITY	THIS CLASS	MAXIMUM POSSIBILITY
	THINKING SEEING LISTENING DOING			
	THINKING SEEING LISTENING DOING			
	THINKING SEEING LISTENING DOING			
	THINKING SEEING LISTENING DOING			
	THINKING SEEING LISTENING DOING			
	THINKING SEEING LISTENING DOING			
	THINKING SEEING LISTENING DOING			
	THINKING SEEING LISTENING DOING			

THIS INSTRUCTOR	BROUGHT ME THE MOST...
	EDUCATION
	TEACHING
	FUN
	CHALLENGES

THIS...	BROUGHT ME THE MOST ISSUES
CLASS	
CONCEPT	
LESSON	
INSTRUCTOR	

THIS CLASS	WAS THE MOST...
	EDUCATIONAL
	WORK
	FUN
	BORING

MAXIMUM POSSIBILITY

1) MOTIVATION	2) INSPIRATION	3) HIGHER EDUCATION	4) CAREER	5) DREAM
6) INVENTION	7) INNOVATION	8) NON-PROFIT	9) FORTUNE 500	10) SUPERHERO

HOW WAS SCHOOL TODAY?

DATE:_____

HOW DID YOU GET ALONG WITH PEOPLE?

ALLIES: POSITIVE / NEGATIVE / NEUTRAL

ANNOYANCES: POSITIVE / NEGATIVE / NEUTRAL INSTRUCTORS: POSITIVE / NEGATIVE / NEUTRAL

HOW DID YOU BEHAVE?

SUCCESSES: MAJOR / MINOR / NONE

STRUGGLES: MAJOR / MINOR / NONE

CONFESSIONS: MAJOR / MINOR / NONE

HOW WAS YOUR ENERGY?

MORNING: FULL TANK / HALF TANK / EMPTY   NOON: FULL TANK / HALF TANK / EMPTY

AFTERNOON: FULL TANK / HALF TANK / EMPTY

DID YOU NEED THE NURSE?

HEALTH: YES / NO   INJURY: YES / NO   PAIN: YES / NO

HOW WAS THE FOOD?

BREAKFAST: DELICIOUS / DECENT / DISGUSTING / DIDN'T EAT

LUNCH: DELICIOUS / DECENT / DISGUSTING / DIDN'T EAT

SNACKS: DELICIOUS / DECENT / DISGUSTING / DIDN'T EAT

QUIET   ANNOYED   COOL   SAD   TIRED   EXCITED   HAPPY   EMBARRASSED   SCARED

BORED   SICK   FRUSTRATED   ANGRY   FUNNY   PROUD   NERVOUS   GOOFY   SURPRISED

B = BEST PART OF YOUR DAY   W = WORST PART OF YOUR DAY   M = MOST OF THE DAY

RECORD IT
WHAT DID YOU LEARN TODAY?

1) ABILITY	2) SKILL	3) VOCATION	4) RELATIONSHIP	5) MENTALITY
6) MENTAL EXERCISE	7) MUSCLE MEMORY	8) PRACTICE	9) TRAINING	10) EXPERIENCE

IN THIS CLASS	I ENGAGED MOST BY ...	MINIMUM FUNCTIONALITY	THIS CLASS	MAXIMUM POSSIBILITY
	THINKING SEEING LISTENING DOING			
	THINKING SEEING LISTENING DOING			
	THINKING SEEING LISTENING DOING			
	THINKING SEEING LISTENING DOING			
	THINKING SEEING LISTENING DOING			
	THINKING SEEING LISTENING DOING			
	THINKING SEEING LISTENING DOING			
	THINKING SEEING LISTENING DOING			

THIS INSTRUCTOR	BROUGHT ME THE MOST...
	EDUCATION
	TEACHING
	FUN
	CHALLENGES

THIS...	BROUGHT ME THE MOST ISSUES
CLASS	
CONCEPT	
LESSON	
INSTRUCTOR	

THIS CLASS	WAS THE MOST...
	EDUCATIONAL
	WORK
	FUN
	BORING

MAXIMUM POSSIBILITY

1) MOTIVATION	2) INSPIRATION	3) HIGHER EDUCATION	4) CAREER	5) DREAM
6) INVENTION	7) INNOVATION	8) NON-PROFIT	9) FORTUNE 500	10) SUPERHERO

HOW WAS SCHOOL TODAY?

DATE:_____

HOW DID YOU GET ALONG WITH PEOPLE?

ALLIES: POSITIVE / NEGATIVE / NEUTRAL

ANNOYANCES: POSITIVE / NEGATIVE / NEUTRAL   INSTRUCTORS: POSITIVE / NEGATIVE / NEUTRAL

HOW DID YOU BEHAVE?

SUCCESSES: MAJOR / MINOR / NONE

STRUGGLES: MAJOR / MINOR / NONE

CONFESSIONS: MAJOR / MINOR / NONE

HOW WAS YOUR ENERGY?

MORNING: FULL TANK / HALF TANK / EMPTY   NOON: FULL TANK / HALF TANK / EMPTY

AFTERNOON: FULL TANK / HALF TANK / EMPTY

DID YOU NEED THE NURSE?

HEALTH: YES / NO   INJURY: YES / NO   PAIN: YES / NO

HOW WAS THE FOOD?

BREAKFAST: DELICIOUS / DECENT / DISGUSTING / DIDN'T EAT

LUNCH: DELICIOUS / DECENT / DISGUSTING / DIDN'T EAT

SNACKS: DELICIOUS / DECENT / DISGUSTING / DIDN'T EAT

QUIET   ANNOYED   COOL   SAD   TIRED   EXCITED   HAPPY   EMBARRASSED   SCARED

BORED   SICK   FRUSTRATED   ANGRY   FUNNY   PROUD   NERVOUS   GOOFY   SURPRISED

B = BEST PART OF YOUR DAY   **W** = WORST PART OF YOUR DAY   **M** = MOST OF THE DAY

RECORD IT
WHAT DID YOU LEARN TODAY?

MINIMUM FUNCTIONALITY

1) ABILITY	2) SKILL	3) VOCATION	4) RELATIONSHIP	5) MENTALITY
6) MENTAL EXERCISE	7) MUSCLE MEMORY	8) PRACTICE	9) TRAINING	10) EXPERIENCE

IN THIS CLASS	I ENGAGED MOST BY ...	MINIMUM FUNCTIONALITY	THIS CLASS	MAXIMUM POSSIBILITY
	THINKING SEEING LISTENING DOING			
	THINKING SEEING LISTENING DOING			
	THINKING SEEING LISTENING DOING			
	THINKING SEEING LISTENING DOING			
	THINKING SEEING LISTENING DOING			
	THINKING SEEING LISTENING DOING			
	THINKING SEEING LISTENING DOING			
	THINKING SEEING LISTENING DOING			

THIS INSTRUCTOR	BROUGHT ME THE MOST...
	EDUCATION
	TEACHING
	FUN
	CHALLENGES

THIS...	BROUGHT ME THE MOST ISSUES
CLASS	
CONCEPT	
LESSON	
INSTRUCTOR	

THIS CLASS	WAS THE MOST...
	EDUCATIONAL
	WORK
	FUN
	BORING

MAXIMUM POSSIBILITY

1) MOTIVATION	2) INSPIRATION	3) HIGHER EDUCATION	4) CAREER	5) DREAM
6) INVENTION	7) INNOVATION	8) NON-PROFIT	9) FORTUNE 500	10) SUPERHERO

HOW WAS SCHOOL TODAY?

DATE:_____

HOW DID YOU GET ALONG WITH PEOPLE?

ALLIES: POSITIVE / NEGATIVE / NEUTRAL

ANNOYANCES: POSITIVE / NEGATIVE / NEUTRAL   INSTRUCTORS: POSITIVE / NEGATIVE / NEUTRAL

HOW DID YOU BEHAVE?

SUCCESSES: MAJOR / MINOR / NONE

STRUGGLES: MAJOR / MINOR / NONE

CONFESSIONS: MAJOR / MINOR / NONE

HOW WAS YOUR ENERGY?

MORNING: FULL TANK / HALF TANK / EMPTY   NOON: FULL TANK / HALF TANK / EMPTY

AFTERNOON: FULL TANK / HALF TANK / EMPTY

DID YOU NEED THE NURSE?

HEALTH: YES / NO   INJURY: YES / NO   PAIN: YES / NO

HOW WAS THE FOOD?

BREAKFAST: DELICIOUS / DECENT / DISGUSTING / DIDN'T EAT

LUNCH: DELICIOUS / DECENT / DISGUSTING / DIDN'T EAT

SNACKS: DELICIOUS / DECENT / DISGUSTING / DIDN'T EAT

QUIET   ANNOYED   COOL   SAD   TIRED   EXCITED   HAPPY   EMBARRASSED   SCARED

BORED   SICK   FRUSTRATED   ANGRY   FUNNY   PROUD   NERVOUS   GOOFY   SURPRISED

B = BEST PART OF YOUR DAY   W = WORST PART OF YOUR DAY   M = MOST OF THE DAY

RECORD IT
WHAT DID YOU LEARN TODAY?

MINIMUM FUNCTIONALITY

1) ABILITY	2) SKILL	3) VOCATION	4) RELATIONSHIP	5) MENTALITY
6) MENTAL EXERCISE	7) MUSCLE MEMORY	8) PRACTICE	9) TRAINING	10) EXPERIENCE

IN THIS CLASS	I ENGAGED MOST BY ...	MINIMUM FUNCTIONALITY	THIS CLASS	MAXIMUM POSSIBILITY
	THINKING SEEING LISTENING DOING			
	THINKING SEEING LISTENING DOING			
	THINKING SEEING LISTENING DOING			
	THINKING SEEING LISTENING DOING			
	THINKING SEEING LISTENING DOING			
	THINKING SEEING LISTENING DOING			
	THINKING SEEING LISTENING DOING			
	THINKING SEEING LISTENING DOING			

THIS INSTRUCTOR	BROUGHT ME THE MOST...
	EDUCATION
	TEACHING
	FUN
	CHALLENGES

THIS...	BROUGHT ME THE MOST ISSUES
CLASS	
CONCEPT	
LESSON	
INSTRUCTOR	

THIS CLASS	WAS THE MOST...
	EDUCATIONAL
	WORK
	FUN
	BORING

MAXIMUM POSSIBILITY

1) MOTIVATION	2) INSPIRATION	3) HIGHER EDUCATION	4) CAREER	5) DREAM
6) INVENTION	7) INNOVATION	8) NON-PROFIT	9) FORTUNE 500	10) SUPERHERO

HOW WAS SCHOOL TODAY?

DATE: _____

HOW DID YOU GET ALONG WITH PEOPLE?

ALLIES: POSITIVE / NEGATIVE / NEUTRAL

ANNOYANCES: POSITIVE / NEGATIVE / NEUTRAL   INSTRUCTORS: POSITIVE / NEGATIVE / NEUTRAL

HOW DID YOU BEHAVE?

SUCCESSES: MAJOR / MINOR / NONE

STRUGGLES: MAJOR / MINOR / NONE

CONFESSIONS: MAJOR / MINOR / NONE

HOW WAS YOUR ENERGY?

MORNING: FULL TANK / HALF TANK / EMPTY   NOON: FULL TANK / HALF TANK / EMPTY

AFTERNOON: FULL TANK / HALF TANK / EMPTY

DID YOU NEED THE NURSE?

HEALTH: YES / NO   INJURY: YES / NO   PAIN: YES / NO

HOW WAS THE FOOD?

BREAKFAST: DELICIOUS / DECENT / DISGUSTING / DIDN'T EAT

LUNCH: DELICIOUS / DECENT / DISGUSTING / DIDN'T EAT

SNACKS: DELICIOUS / DECENT / DISGUSTING / DIDN'T EAT

QUIET   ANNOYED   COOL   SAD   TIRED   EXCITED   HAPPY   EMBARRASSED   SCARED

BORED   SICK   FRUSTRATED   ANGRY   FUNNY   PROUD   NERVOUS   GOOFY   SURPRISED

B = BEST PART OF YOUR DAY   **W** = WORST PART OF YOUR DAY   **M** = MOST OF THE DAY

RECORD IT
WHAT DID YOU LEARN TODAY?

MINIMUM FUNCTIONALITY

1) ABILITY	2) SKILL	3) VOCATION	4) RELATIONSHIP	5) MENTALITY
6) MENTAL EXERCISE	7) MUSCLE MEMORY	8) PRACTICE	9) TRAINING	10) EXPERIENCE

IN THIS CLASS	I ENGAGED MOST BY ...	MINIMUM FUNCTIONALITY	THIS CLASS	MAXIMUM POSSIBILITY
	THINKING SEEING LISTENING DOING			
	THINKING SEEING LISTENING DOING			
	THINKING SEEING LISTENING DOING			
	THINKING SEEING LISTENING DOING			
	THINKING SEEING LISTENING DOING			
	THINKING SEEING LISTENING DOING			
	THINKING SEEING LISTENING DOING			
	THINKING SEEING LISTENING DOING			

THIS INSTRUCTOR	BROUGHT ME THE MOST...
	EDUCATION
	TEACHING
	FUN
	CHALLENGES

THIS...	BROUGHT ME THE MOST ISSUES
CLASS	
CONCEPT	
LESSON	
INSTRUCTOR	

THIS CLASS	WAS THE MOST...
	EDUCATIONAL
	WORK
	FUN
	BORING

MAXIMUM POSSIBILITY

1) MOTIVATION	2) INSPIRATION	3) HIGHER EDUCATION	4) CAREER	5) DREAM
6) INVENTION	7) INNOVATION	8) NON-PROFIT	9) FORTUNE 500	10) SUPERHERO

PROGRESS REPORT

1) When I think about my interactions with people this quarter, I see that:
   I was successful…_____
   _____
   I really struggled…_____
   _____
   Moving forward…_____
   _____
   I may need my allies…_____
   _____

2) When I think about my behavior this quarter, I see that:
   I was successful…_____
   _____
   I really struggled…_____
   _____
   Moving forward…_____
   _____
   I may need my allies…_____
   _____

3) When I think about my overall health this quarter, I see that:
   I was successful…_____
   _____
   I really struggled…_____
   _____
   Moving forward…_____
   _____
   I may need my allies…_____
   _____

4) When I think about my eating habits this quarter, I see that:
   I was successful…_____
   _____
   I really struggled…_____
   _____
   Moving forward…_____
   _____
   I may need my allies…_____
   _____

5) When I think about my overall experience in school this quarter, I see that:
   I was successful…_____
   _____
   I really struggled…_____
   _____
   Moving forward…_____
   _____
   I may need my allies…_____
   _____

PROGRESS REPORT

6) When I think about how I engaged in classes this quarter, I see that:
I was successful…_____
_____

I really struggled…_____
_____

Moving forward…_____
_____

I may need my allies…_____
_____

7) When I think about the educational value of class experiences this quarter, I see that:
I was successful…_____
_____

I really struggled…_____
_____

Moving forward…_____
_____

I may need my allies…_____
_____

8) When I think about how my instructors did this quarter, I see that:
I was successful…_____
_____

I really struggled…_____
_____

Moving forward…_____
_____

I may need my allies…_____
_____

9) When I think about academic issues I had this quarter, I see that:
I was successful…_____
_____

I really struggled…_____
_____

Moving forward…_____
_____

I may need my allies…_____
_____

10) When I think about how my classes went this quarter, I see that:
I was successful…_____
_____

I really struggled…_____
_____

Moving forward…_____
_____

I may need my allies…_____
_____

GLOSSARY OF TERMS

Accountable – being anchored by and firmly attached to an obligation or responsibility.

Active Participant – student persona resembling a permissive readiness to observe the instruction of educational leadership energetically and optimistically in hopes of acquiring a high-quality education.

Adolescence – a transitional phase, between childhood and adulthood, where one's ability to prove they can control and be responsible for their life, by doing things appropriately and efficiently with a high probability of success, allows those with partial control and responsibility for their life and livelihood to give up control and responsibility fully.

Adolescent – one who has attained limited control and responsibility for their life and livelihood because of increased learning, understanding, maturing, education in the study of life, and the limited ability to do things appropriately and efficiently with a good probability of success.

Adult – one who has attained full control and responsibility for their life and livelihood because of superior learning, understanding, maturing, education in the study of life, and the ability to do things appropriately and efficiently with a high probability of success.

Adulthood – a phase of life after adolescence where superior learning, understanding, maturing, education in the study of life, and the ability to do things appropriately and efficiently with a high probability of success allow one to have full control and responsibility for their life and livelihood.

Advocate – the recognition of a position of weakness and vulnerability paired with an offering of supportive actions meant to defend and protect.

Ally – an individual, entity, or institution that has a joint interest and agrees to partner with another in their pursuit of a goal.

Authority – having the permission or being in the position to deny or grant the allowance of using power.

Caregiver – one who is focused on fulfilling the basic needs of a child.

Certified – considered to be educated by an officially authorized governing body or agency in a particular area or field of study.

GLOSSARY OF TERMS

Child – one whose life and livelihood are the responsibility of another more than they are for themself, because of their need for learning, understanding, maturing, and an education in the study of life.

Childhood – a transitional phase in a child's life, before adolescence, where the exploration of curiosity leads to learning, understanding, maturing, and an education in the study of life that prompts those responsible for their life and livelihood to give them limited control and responsibility over their own life.

Classroom Management – a teacher's ability to assess how well the academic environment provides space and opportunity for the exposure to, exploration of, and experience with an education, and steer experiences away from low levels of effectiveness while pushing toward higher levels.

Demand – to make an official request from a position of authority and refuse to be denied.

Discipline – the process of putting someone under control.

Education – a unique assortment of information that one possesses, understands, knows how to use, and benefits from (qualitatively).

Educate – to take the lead in a focused effort to assist students in their pursuit of an education.

Educated – possessing qualitative evidence of an acquired education.

Educator – one who, intentionally, teaches lessons and plans activities that allow students to be exposed to, explore, and experience an education to provoke and support them in pursuing and acquiring an education.

Educational Value Continuum™ – a scale that documents and expresses how one could use and benefit from a variety of functions and possibilities contained within academic information once that content has been possessed and understood.

Engaged Agent – student persona embodying an acute preparation to adhere to the educational process eagerly and expectantly with aspirations of acquiring full mastery of the educational possibility.

GLOSSARY OF TERMS

Fun – enjoyment of an experience.

Graduate – one who is ready, prepared, and qualified for an advanced educational level by becoming certified as a successful student on the previous learning level.

Grievance – a specific complaint filed with righteous authority for the purpose of solving a problem.

Hypocrisy – professing a standard or belief that one's character or behavior fails to support.

Influence – the persuasive energy of one's power, authority, and/or resources that act on or prompt another.

Integrity – having thoughts, words, and actions that all resemble the same thing.

Intense Trainer – educator persona exemplifying astute intuition while demonstrating supreme proficiency and mastery of a high-quality education.

Miseducation of Education™ – an endemic issue plaguing the education system caused by a failure to explicitly define "education," which produces and perpetuates obstructions to the productivity, possibility, and promise of the system: disallowing any assurance that progression through an institution's academic program is purposed for acquiring an education.

Noble – held and regarded in a class or rank esteemed highly above others because of one's distinguished excellence.

Parent – one who takes responsibility for a child's life, livelihood, growth, and development while providing safe, appropriate space and opportunity for that child to explore their curiosity while becoming more knowledgeable and experienced in areas where learning, understanding, and maturing are necessary.

Power – the ability to do.

Prepared – fulfillment of the internal and external prerequisites necessary to accomplish a thing.

GLOSSARY OF TERMS

Profound Mentor – educator persona exhibiting keen insight while demonstrating practical integration of a high-quality education.

Pupil – one who is willing to submit to instruction and participate in learning.

Qualified – possessing educational abilities and evidence that project and predict probable success.

Ready – acknowledgment of an internal desire and willingness to accomplish a thing.

Righteous Authority – being properly positioned with and connected to a higher source of authority and, thereby, permitted to allow or deny the usage of power to those dependent upon you.

School – a designated area that provides space and opportunity to be exposed to, explore, and experience an education.

Student – one who actively engages in the pursuit of an education.

Success – the achievement/accomplishment of one's goal(s).

Teaching – the utilization of knowledgeable lessons and/or activities to instruct an intellectual minor in an academic discipline, practical ability, or vocational skill set.

Teacher – one who provides an intellectual minor with an understanding of knowledge previously unfamiliar through teaching.

ABOUT THE AUTHOR

Daniel C. Manley is an American educator, author, speaker, and educational provocateur who has made it his life's work to make the attainment of a high-quality education a real possibility for all young people. As a mentor, teacher, and administrator, he has served the middle school and high school population for nearly twenty years. As Co-Founder and CEO of Stand & Withstand Integrity Group, he has made it his mission to empower and prepare children to be firmly planted, deeply rooted, and properly positioned as adults with an education that allows for them to achieve practical success.

Coming Soon
SUPPLY IT:
What "Teaching Is A Noble Profession" Really Means

USE IT & BENEFIT:
Functions & Possibilities of an Education Series

For Booking
Stand & Withstand Integrity Group LLC
P.O. Box 782771
Wichita, KS 67278

CONTACT@STANDWITHSTAND.ORG

CPSIA information can be obtained
at www.ICGtesting.com
Printed in the USA
BVHW011411021121
620550BV00015B/698